BIRDING WITH YEATS

BIRDING

WITH

YEATS

A MEMOIR

LYNN
THOMSON

ANANSI

This edition published in 2014 by
House of Anansi Press Inc.
110 Spadina Avenue, Suite 801
Toronto, ON, M5V 2K4
Tel. 416-363-4343
Fax 416-363-1017
www.houseofanansi.com

Distributed in Canada by
HarperCollins Canada Ltd.
1995 Markham Road
Scarborough, ON, M1B 5M8
Toll free tel. 1-800-387-0117

Distributed in the United States by
Publishers Group West
1700 Fourth Street
Berkeley, CA 94710
Toll free tel. 1-800-788-3123

House of Anansi Press is committed to protecting our natural environment.
As part of our efforts, the interior of this book is printed on paper that contains 100% post-
consumer recycled fibres, is acid-free, and is processed chlorine-free.

18 17 16 15 14 1 2 3 4 5

Library and Archives Canada Cataloguing in Publication

Thomson, Lynn, 1960–, author
Birding with Yeats: a memoir / Lynn Thomson.

Issued in print and electronic formats.
ISBN 978-1-77089-389-4 (pbk.).—ISBN 978-1-77089-390-0 (epub)

1. Thomson, Lynn, 1960–. 2. Thomson, Lynn, 1960– —Family.
3. Mothers and sons. 4. Birdwatching. I. Title.

HQ799.15.T46 2014 649'.125 C2013-906999-2
C2013-907000-1

Library of Congress Control Number: 2013918882

Jacket design: Alysia Shewchuk
Text design and typesetting: Alysia Shewchuk
The image on pages ii–iii is courtesy of Barbara Stoneham.
The maps on pages vii–xii are by Alysia Shewchuk.

*We acknowledge for their financial support of our publishing program
the Canada Council for the Arts, the Ontario Arts Council, and the Government of Canada
through the Canada Book Fund.*

Printed and bound in Canada

MIX
Paper from
responsible sources
FSC® C016245

For Ben and Yeats

VANCOUVER
ISLAND

PACIFIC OCEAN

Comox

Cathedral
Grove

Tofino

Kennedy Lake

Nanaimo

De Courcy
Island

Salt Spring
Island

Victoria

N

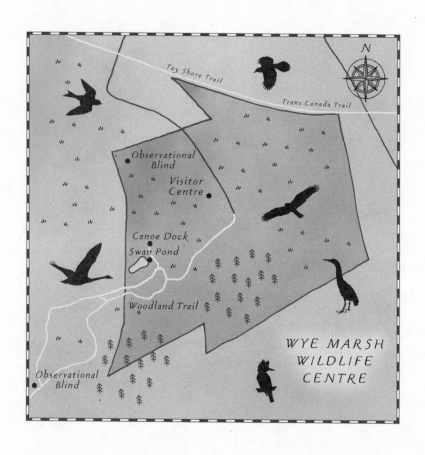

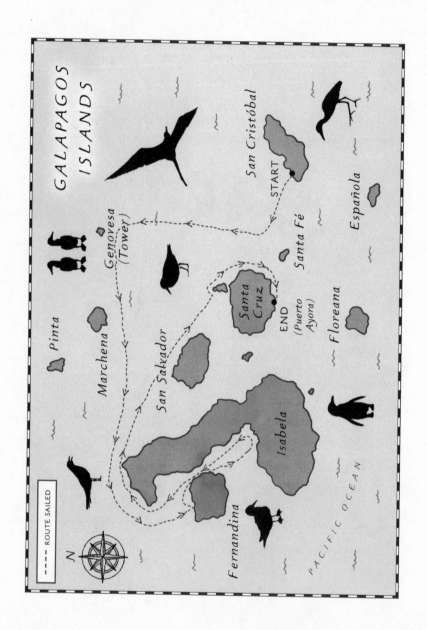

GALAPAGOS ISLANDS

- - - ROUTE SAILED

N

Pinta

Marchena

Genovesa (Tower)

San Salvador

San Cristóbal

START

Santa Fé

Santa Cruz

END (Puerto Ayora)

Floreana

Española

Fernandina

Isabela

PACIFIC OCEAN

POINT
PELEE

Marsh
Boardwalk

Blue
Heron

LAKE
ERIE

Dunes

DeLaurier
Homestead
& Trail

Visitor
Centre

Woodland
Nature
Trail

Tip

Leamington

Hillman
Marsh

N

Point
Pelee

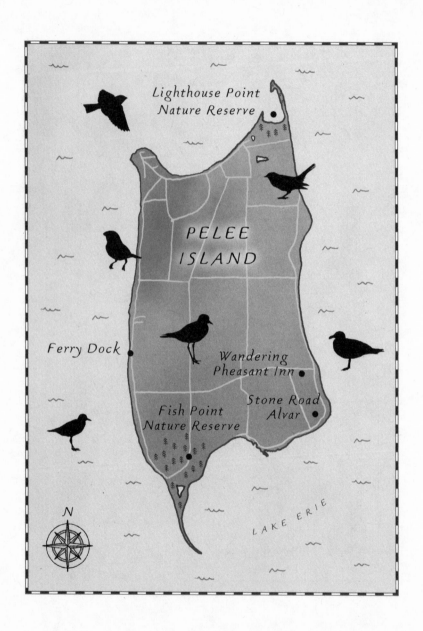

Lighthouse Point
Nature Reserve

PELEE
ISLAND

Ferry Dock

Wandering
Pheasant Inn

Stone Road
Alvar

Fish Point
Nature Reserve

LAKE ERIE

N

Around me the trees stir in their leaves
and call out, "Stay awhile."
The light flows from their branches.

And they call again, "It's simple," they say,
"and you too have come
into the world to do this, to go easy, to be filled
with light, and to shine."

Mary Oliver, from "When I Am Among the Trees"

PROLOGUE

IF I SIT IN a forest thick with pines and pay close attention to the sound of every living thing, I feel as though my heart might split open. I put my ear to a clump of moss and hear the Earth breathe. There are a billion little creatures chewing in the leaf mould, a billion tiny wings whirring under the blackberry thicket. When I lie down in the tall grass, I hear this and I'm slowly consumed by the press of nature.

I come out of the forest on top of a hill and into a meadow of sumac and juniper. The smell is different here; the heat feels different. These small trees give off such a different vibration from those tall pines. In a pine forest in the wind, all the sound is high up in the treetops, whooshing and sighing. Ferns on the forest floor, green and straining towards the light, give off their own slightly bitter aroma.

If I left this place for the tropics, with all those dripping, viney trees, would I long eternally for the pines? Would I lie in bed at night listening to the howler monkeys scream and feel the longing spin through every cell of my body? Would I fall asleep with the smell of frangipani enveloping me and wake with the scent of pine on my skin?

And I haven't even mentioned the birds! The chickadees alone, with their incessant *deedeedee*, can rattle my senses, not to mention the nuthatches and the downy woodpeckers *peck-peck-pecking* at the trees.

I find that when I really pay attention, I'll remember which bird I'm hearing (sounds almost like a robin, must be a red-eyed vireo), which bird that is with the black-and-yellow head (Blackburnian warbler), and which tiny bird is scratching away under the forsythia (house wren). But if my attention is caught up in other things, the bird names don't come as easily. On a depressingly regular basis I'll say to my husband, Ben, "What kind of bird is that?" and he'll say, "That's a squirrel." At the cottage we have red squirrels that can sound like demented blue jays, but I should be able to recognize our city squirrels. It's a good reminder to stay present, instead of allowing my mind to wander and daydream.

Part of the reason my son, Yeats, and I go anywhere is to bird-watch. It has become a habit. We rarely set out on an expedition with the intention of seeing one particular bird species. We just go birdwatching. The act of being outdoors looking for birds, especially ones we've never seen before, is enough. Some people are very competitive in their birding.

Maybe they'll die happy, having seen a thousand species before they die, but I'll die happy knowing I've spent all that quiet time being present.

Sometimes I think that the point of birdwatching is not the actual seeing of the birds, but the cultivation of patience. Of course, each time we set out, there's a certain amount of expectation that we'll see something, maybe even a species we've never seen before, and that it will fill us with light. But even if we don't see anything remarkable — and sometimes that happens — we come home filled with light anyway.

Birding complements Yeats's personality — his patience, his calmness, his drive to make lists, and his fabulous memory. It also complements his desire to be in the natural world, to see beautiful things, and to seek deeper meaning about our place as a species on this earth.

I think the most important quality in a birdwatcher is a willingness to stand quietly and see what comes. Our everyday lives obscure a truth about existence — that at the heart of everything there lies a stillness and a light.

ONE

IT WAS BEN WHO taught me the basics of birdwatching, early in our relationship. He took me across the footbridge over the Don Valley Parkway, in the east end of Toronto, to a place called Riverdale Farm. The farm was once Toronto's first zoo, but in 1974 it became a working farm with domestic animals like Shorthorn cows, Cotswold sheep, and Nubian goats. It was a fifteen-minute walk from our apartment and a refuge from the busy city that surrounds it.

We stood by a wild patch of ground beside a chain-link fence that separated the farm from the Bayview Avenue extension. Cars roared past, hidden from view. The farm animals were up the hill in the corrals and barns. We were alone down there, near the pond, hiding behind a little patch of land all covered in bushes. We stood stock-still and waited.

On those beginner expeditions we saw red-winged blackbirds, American robins, black-capped chickadees, dark-eyed juncos, and various sparrows and warblers. I'd always loved sparrows and was surprised to learn that there were so many varieties. Around Toronto you can find roughly fifteen kinds if you're lucky and patient and know where to look.

Back then, in the middle of the pond at Riverdale Farm, there was an island big enough for one small tree, some grasses, and one Canada goose nest. Every spring we went to the farm to watch one goose sit on her nest while the other geese swam around the pond. We stood on the little bridge and looked for giant orange carp in the water and for painted turtles basking in the sun on half-submerged logs. A great blue heron would stalk by on its long legs, eye out for frogs or fish, and we would hold our breath.

I became pregnant about a year after Ben and I moved into that apartment on Riverdale Avenue, just across the valley from the farm. We moved again, this time into a house, and six weeks later I gave birth to a beautiful baby. It took us a little while to name Yeats. I remember when he was four days old I was nursing him in bed and Ben came into the room.

He regarded us for a moment and said, "How about Yeats?"

I looked down at my bald baby and said, "That's perfect!"

Yeats was named after the Irish poet but also after one of Ben's oldest friends whose middle name was Yates. This friend had lived on an ashram in India for more than thirty years. Yeats's middle name came from another one of Ben's old friends, whose surname was Pinto. Yeats Pinto McNally—a good Irish name.

We took baby Yeats to Riverdale Farm along with my three stepchildren, Titus, Rupert, and Danielle. The kids loved going to the farm to see the baby goats and chicks, and to run up and down the unpaved pathways. Baby Yeats loved doing anything when his brothers and sister were around, but Riverdale Farm was a special place for all of us. We felt like we were out of the city as soon as we passed through its gate.

One time, when Yeats was a toddler, we visited the farm with our old friend Chris.

We were standing at a railing looking out over a boggy area, hoping to see ducks, when Chris said, "Look! A yellow-headed blackbird!"

He pointed into the scrub and we all saw it: a bird the shape and size of a red-winged blackbird but with a golden head.

I said, "Chris, are you a closet birdwatcher?"

He said, "Nah. I just know a yellow-headed blackbird when I see one."

His eyes were twinkling. I scratched my head.

He said, "I don't think those birds are supposed to come here, to Toronto." We looked back at the bird. Yeats was jumping up and down.

"Accidentals" are birds that are far from their normal range and that have been sighted only rarely in the area. Sometimes decades or even centuries will go between sightings. Birders will call accidentals in to their local birding club or to the National Audubon Society, who will send someone to confirm the sighting. I don't know for sure that we saw the yellow-headed blackbird that day and sometimes I question our identification. Those birds aren't supposed to come any-where near here, being from the West. Yeats was too young to remember, so it hasn't been checked off his list.

THAT EARLY EXPEDITION TO Riverdale Farm was around the time when Yeats discovered the *Audubon Society Field Guide to North American Birds*. We all spent hours going through that book. Yeats still spends hours poring over bird guides, the more detail the better.

Even then, as a toddler, he would clamber onto my lap (or Ben's lap, or Uncle Greg's lap...) and slide the ever-present guide in front of me. We'd start at the beginning with the very first bird, the snowy egret, underneath which is the great egret, and beside those, the reddish egret and the cattle egret. He'd point at the birds and I'd say their names, turn the page, and continue on through 584 birds until we reached the black-billed magpie at the end. Sometimes we'd finish and he'd say, "Again," and back we'd go to the egrets.

A couple of years later he wanted me to read bits from the back section of the book — habitats, nesting behaviours, and so on — but never with the same linear dedication we applied to the photographs. Yeats must have gone through that book with some willing adult or other a hundred times. Two hundred times. A thousand times.

We still have that copy of the book, and one segment—
from the prothonotary warbler to the Philadelphia vireo—is
threatening to disengage from the binding. We use it only
rarely now, to make a quick backyard bird identification at
the kitchen table.

"Is it a house finch or a purple finch?"

The females of these two birds look exactly the same and
the males differ only slightly, as far as I can tell, with the purple finch being...more purple. I need to check the book to be
sure of what I'm seeing.

WE BEGAN READING TO Yeats when he was an infant, newly
sentient. We are booksellers and our house is full of books. I
read to Yeats when he wasn't sleeping or eating or watching
dust motes in the sunshine. I read to him every single day
(unless I was out of town or Yeats was at a sleep-over) until he
was sixteen years old. Sometimes he laments that I never read
to him anymore, and sometimes I do read to him. Sometimes
he now reads to me, but not very often.

I started with whatever I had at hand—a newspaper,
a magazine, a book of short stories. But when he was old
enough to sit in my lap and look at the books, we took up children's picture books. We read everything, from *Sylvester and
the Magic Pebble* to the Thomas the Tank Engine stories to
The Story About Ping to Rupert Bear annuals. (I still remember the rhyming couplet from a Rupert story: "My name is
Dickon of the Dell. / There waits my horse, he serves me

well.") Some days we'd spend three or four hours reading, interspersed with meals and visits to the park and playing on the floor. It was something I could do even while completely exhausted.

And I was often completely exhausted. Yeats was born at the end of July, during a heat wave. He nursed all the time. Though the weather eventually settled, the nursing seemed to go on forever, every three hours. I had dreamed of reading while breastfeeding, but after trying two or three times, I set that dream aside. Yeats wanted to lock eyes with me while he fed and became very cranky very quickly if he couldn't. For me, this eye contact was so rewarding that now I can't imagine why I had wanted to read instead.

As a baby, Yeats didn't sleep for more than three hours at a time, day or night. I'd decided on the on-demand nursing regime. I nursed him when he was hungry, not according to my own schedule. My mom thought I was crazy. She had all three of her babies on a schedule as soon as we were born, and we were "good" about it. I read some books and talked to some people and decided against the schedule, and because I was the mother this time, Mom kept quiet. She called me every day, though, to see how much sleep I'd had the night before. I wanted to scream. I was exhausted. I was cranky. I napped when Yeats napped and none of the housework got done. Ben woke with him at night, but Yeats wanted me, not his father.

Titus, Rupert, and Danielle came over every other weekend and one night every week. Danielle, three years old, cuddled her baby brother on the couch. The boys were curious but wary. Titus was twelve already, a bit old to engage with a baby brother, and besides, he preferred to be with his friends. Rupert was nearly six, and more of a homebody. He'd always wanted desperately to be friends with Titus, and though he now had another brother, this one was a baby and it wasn't the same. We sat Yeats in his chair on the floor and the older kids played around him. He squealed and screamed and loved every minute of it. For these hours he had siblings, and for the rest of the time he was an only child.

Because of the age difference, Titus didn't accompany us on many expeditions. He'd opt for an overnight at a friend's house instead of an early morning jaunt to the zoo, for example. But as everyone grew older, the four children found more in common, especially a love of reading, and they became not only friends, but staunch supporters and defenders of one another.

The summer Yeats turned one, we all learned something elemental about him, something that has coloured the way I see my son, and what I read to him, to this day. We were at the cottage with my family — my sister, Laurie, and her husband, Andy; my brother, Greg (who had yet to meet Sarah, his future wife); and my mother, Nancy — taking turns reading nursery rhymes aloud around the breakfast table. Laurie read "Little Bo Peep, she lost her sheep..." Ben read "Little Jack Horner sat in a corner..." I started in with "Three little kittens, they lost their mittens..." When I reached the part where the mother cat says, "Lost your mittens, you naughty kittens, then you shall have no pie," Yeats began to howl. I stopped reading. My mother, who was sitting beside him, said, "It's okay, Yeats. Don't worry. The mommy cat loves her kittens." She calmed him down.

I recited "Hey diddle diddle, the cat and the fiddle" instead, but when it came to my brother's turn, he said the kitten one again. Everything was fine until the line about "you naughty kittens," when Yeats burst into tears again. Greg stopped reading and Yeats stopped crying. Someone else around the table said the rhyme again, and again Yeats cried on cue. People laughed and someone made it happen again. Before this became a party trick and started making me angry, I said, "Will you all stop torturing my child? I know it's funny, but can't you see how upset he is?" Yeats's face remained a study in misery until Mom rubbed his back and whispered yet again that the mother cat really did love her kittens.

He obviously couldn't abide the thought of anyone getting into that kind of trouble—and the thing is, as he grew into an older child and eventually into a teen, he rarely got into that kind of trouble himself. If he did, he was repentant with all his heart.

For most of my family, this was their first glimpse of Yeats's sensitivity and a small taste of the challenge he would present to us of how to live in this world.

POETRY, TOO, WAS A way of life for Yeats. As a toddler, when Yeats was in the bath, I read him adult poetry. I read him Shakespeare; he especially liked the witches from *Macbeth* and asked that I read "Double, double toil and trouble / Fire burn and cauldron bubble" to him over and over again. I read him Rossetti and Tennyson and Michael Ondaatje. I read him whatever we had lying around the house (yes, even W. B. Yeats), and he soaked it all up.

I have an old, battered paperback edition of Robert Frost poems that has lived in our bathroom for eighteen years now. Yeats loved those poems. I read one about apple trees and birds and he sat listening. When I finished he said, "Again!" and I would go back to the beginning. I read "The Road Not Taken" and "The Sound of Trees." He sat bug-eyed in the bath. When Yeats was five years old we memorized "Stopping By Woods on a Snowy Evening" for my aunt and uncle's Christmas-party talent show and recited it together to wild applause.

One day, when we were playing in the front yard, a neighbour stopped by to chat. Yeats was pushing his little plastic rake back and forth across the lawn while reciting a poem, something he was making up on the spot. The neighbour said, "He sounds like Robert Frost," and I felt a thrill in my bones.

When Yeats began reading to himself at night, continuing on alone after Ben or I had read to him, one of his early favourites was Shel Silverstein. He read poem after poem until he dropped off to sleep with the book still open on the bed.

As an adolescent, too, Yeats was an avid poetry reader. He always had two or three books of poetry lying around his bedroom. One summer he read the entire canon of W. B. Yeats. The next summer, it was Longfellow. And he wrote his own poetry, too. He wouldn't let us read what he wrote, but we had it from a reliable source that he was good. We were not surprised to learn that a lot of it was about the natural world.

Ben thought it was partly the poet in Yeats that drew him to birdwatching. These two pursuits, for him, at least, were solitary. They required long periods of time in seeming reflection, quiet, and stillness. They asked for his patience as he waited for something to come — an image, a bird, an inspiration.

Birds are everywhere in our literature, a part, it seems, of our collective poetic imagination. If writing a beautiful line of poetry fills a poet's heart with joy, imagine how that same poet's soul must take flight at the sight of swallows soaring through the evening sky!

I saw that happen with my son. I'd ask him what the matter was and he'd say, "I need to write. I haven't written for a while." He'd get up from the chair and pace around a bit. "Maybe I'll go birdwatching," he'd say, reaching for his binoculars. The two activities were linked — writing poetry and birdwatching.

FROM THE TIME YEATS was three years old until he started high school, we spent our entire summers up North, in Muskoka. My mother was there, and Greg came on weekends. My sister Laurie and her husband lived in London, England until 2003, when they moved to Greenwich, Connecticut, and she brought her family to Muskoka for the summers, too. Summertime was when we all reconnected and created a stockpile of family stories.

We took Yeats to the cottage for the first time when he was two weeks old. I have a photograph of us on the dock under a shade umbrella. Laurie is holding Yeats, and he appears to be glowering at her, closely studying this woman who looks *almost* like his mother. I'm sitting in a chaise next to them looking very relaxed (exhausted) and happy (delirious). I remember an old family friend who lived in Muskoka year-round dropping by to see Yeats and saying, "Another Muskoka baby. It will never leave his blood."

That was how we all felt: steeped in the Canadian Shield.

Cottage life was in my family's blood. My father's family had spent a month every summer at a cottage on a lake in southern Saskatchewan, and my mother spent a month each summer at her grandmother's cottage on Lake Scugog in Ontario. My parents dreamed of a cottage for their family, so they rented one for a month every summer when I was growing up. Usually it was on Lake Rosseau in Muskoka, where friends of theirs also rented.

We went to the same place for eight summers. I remember arriving there every year before the July 1 weekend and rushing into the little boathouse with Laurie and Greg to see if the boat was still above water. We rented an old outboard along with the cottage, and half the time this boat would have become swamped with water from spring storms and ended up sunk. Now that we had a cottage on an island and several boats in a boathouse, it was a mystery to me why that old boat spent so much time at the bottom of the lake, but it was hilarious at the time.

Mom and Dad wanted a cottage of their own, and by the mid-1980s they finally felt they could afford one. In 1986 they bought an island in Lake Rosseau that had a boathouse and an old cottage. The island is called Prospect on the map, but is known locally as "Old Baldy" because half the island is a big round hill of rock. When they bought the cottage, this hill was nearly devoid of vegetation due to a fire many years before. When the island was uninhabited, generations of cottagers had used it for picnics and evening parties and left all kinds of debris. It's surmised that the fire started with sunlight beating down on a piece of glass. The previous owners told us they'd scoured the hill for bits of broken glass, taking off bushel barrels full. But we'd still find the occasional piece of glass there, half-buried and working its way out of the earth.

The vegetation grew up quickly until "Old Baldy" was no longer bald. The hill was soon covered in juniper, poplar, sumac, and oak. We took regular hikes to the top, where we had two fine lookouts over the lake. We were on a "height of land," as my geologist grandfather used to say. From the top of the hill looking south, we could see a couple of small islands with their cottages hidden in the trees, and beyond those, the mainland. On the mainland was the Muskoka Lakes Golf and Country Club, where we parked our cars and picked one another up in the boats. Looking north and east from the top of the hill we could see more islands in the distance, across a large expanse of water. This is where the sun rose. Directly to the west of Baldy was Fairylands Island, which was a much larger island than ours and had nearly a dozen boathouses dotted around its perimeter.

Our cottage was on one of the islands across from that sinky-boat cottage on the mainland, beyond the first row of islands and a little bit west. From our dock we could see the old mustard-coloured boathouse with its one little slip. I stood on our dock staring across the lake at that place where, as a child, I used to stand looking out at this place. I was staring at myself across the years.

Only a couple of years after they bought the island, Dad was diagnosed with colon cancer, and Mom and Dad were divorced. It all seemed to happen at the same time. Dad had only five really good summers at his wonderful island sanctuary, something I still find hard to believe. So much happened in those five years, from a makeover of the boathouse and new landscaping behind the cottage, to my sister's wedding and the start of my relationship with Ben.

Laurie and Andy were married in a little church up the lake at Windermere, and their reception was at the golf club across from the island. The cottage was full of guests that Labour Day weekend of 1991. Exactly one year later, when he was fifty-seven, Dad would have his last weekend up North; just weeks after that, I would be pregnant with Yeats.

Laurie, Greg, Dad, and I sat on the back deck on that final weekend and discussed finances. Dad was leaving us with some money, but it wouldn't last forever. He suggested we each put a certain amount into a designated investment portfolio and use that money for the cottage. He suggested we divvy up the cottage tasks so no one was left doing all the work.

As we listened and talked, Dad was busy picking the dead bits out of a potted plant. He was wearing all white and sat in the sunshine, his grey hair sparse but full of light. His fingers were bony and dry, and so were the little branches he was pulling off the plant. It made my heart break to watch him because really that plant was dead, with one tiny scraggly green growth left, and I knew that by the end of our conversation, there would be nothing left at all.

Dad's last time at the family cottage, Labour Day weekend, 1992, coincided with the first time my stepchildren came up. It was a changing of the guard. I have a strong memory of Danielle, age two and a half, climbing onto Dad's lap, looking up at him with her huge brown eyes, and saying, "You are my best friend."

Dad said, "Already?" and the rest of us laughed. He was weak with chemo and cancer and had barely three months to live, but he engaged with all three children as best he could. He was clearly thrilled to have this sweet little girl on his lap. He would have been a proud and wonderful grandfather.

My sister Laurie built a second cottage on the island when everyone started having children, because instead of dividing up our time at the lake as some families do, we decided we wanted to be there together. The new cottage was on the north side of the island, down a hill and in the trees. Unlike the old cottage, which was a bungalow, it had a lower level and a second storey. Mom had a room of her own downstairs. Her desk had a view of the lake through the trees and sometimes she was surprised by Laurie's son, Thomas, waterskiing past, sending a rooster-tail of spray over the dock. She had a comfortable reading chair and she often slipped away to find some peace and quiet, especially on rainy days when everyone stayed inside.

We built a new dock, too, off the north side of the island. We used this dock for stargazing, since there were no neighbours with lights to interfere with our view of the sky. It was darker and quieter on this side of the island, and the vista was bigger there.

I'd go to the new dock to watch the sunrise, followed by whichever cats were outside. We all brought our cats to Muskoka. At first, Mom and I were the only ones with cats, Dubleau and Simon. Then Greg got Kibo. The cats had to share the old cottage, and they tolerated one another. Dubleau was old so he died first, though not on the island. Then Simon died one summer. He went under the cottage and never came out. I saw him under there, his eyes reflecting light, looking back at me, but he turned away when I called to him. He was fourteen. For a summer there was only Kibo and she slept in a cupboard most of the time.

Then we got Pippin, a male grey tabby, and Laurie's family got Jumper, a female orange tabby. As kittens they were best friends, but when Laurie's family moved from Connecticut to Toronto, their daughter, Lauren, was promised a new kitten. They got Freddy, a male cat who was extremely cute — white with black splotches — but not very smart. Jumper was offended by this addition to her family and took it out on everyone, Pippin included. Then Greg got Smokey, Kibo died, and they got Tigger. Smokey was a Russian Blue and Tigger was orange, and both cats had long, fluffy hair. Smokey was one of those friendly cats who wanted to bring everyone together. He tried and tried to befriend Jumper. He made some headway with Pippin but had to start all over again every summer. Freddy loved all the other cats, but neither Jumper nor Pippin would have anything to do with him, and Tigger was a 'fraidy-cat.

All these cats on the island drove Ben and Yeats crazy. We stopped putting out our bird feeders because the cats would lie in wait.

I'd say, "Look, there are three cats lying in the field. They're so cute."

Ben would say, "You mean so dumb."

Yeats would say, "Too many cats. I can't go anywhere where there isn't a cat."

And that was the truth. If we went to the top of the hill, we'd find Jumper sitting at a lookout, watching over the lake. If I carried the washing up to the clothesline, Pippin would crawl out of the juniper bush and rub against my legs. If we sat on the dock watching the stars come out, Smokey would appear from nowhere.

When I sat on that dew-soaked dock and waited for the sunrise, Jumper and Pippin and Smokey would be sitting a little ways off, also facing east. We were all silent; there were no boats and the lake was still as glass. The cats tipped their noses up to smell the air and a raven swooped down from the forest, silent too except for the whoosh of its wings.

Some mornings the ravens hopped around on the cottage roof right over my head. Inky-black tricksters. They flew from the roof and put up a squawking racket loud enough to wake the dead. Some mornings they hung out together in the thickest part of a tall hemlock tree down by the water. When I went to fetch the newspaper off the dock, they startled and flew, one by one, out of the tree and around the end of the island. "Caw! Caw! Croak!" Six black giants of the air.

Most summers we had nesting blue jays on the island. One time, before we had so many cats, Yeats and I sat at the picnic table on the back deck and counted all the jays we could see. Two at the feeder, two hopping around on the roof above the feeder, two in the birch tree beside us, two on the lowest branch of the pine across the field, and two more in another pine close by. That made ten, until another pair flew in, making a dozen. They were all interested in the feeder.

Blue jays are members of the corvid family, as are crows, ravens, magpies, and other kinds of jays like the Stellar's jay and the grey jay. The corvids have the largest brain-body ratio of all the bird families, making them seem uncannily smart. "Bird brains," indeed.

When we listened carefully we could hear the jays communicating with each other. That morning they weren't engaged in their raucous *Thief! Thief!* call, but in their gentle *psh psh psh*. We could hear the pair in the birch tree talking like this, back and forth, gentle and sweet. Imitating this sound was a good way to call a curious blue jay down from its tree. Make the sound, wait, do it again. The blue jay would hop to a closer branch, cock its head to look at you, and make its *psh psh psh* sound back at you. You made the sound again; it hopped closer and cocked its head.

Once I was sitting on the back deck and I started calling down a blue jay. It was advancing slowly, branch by branch, through a pine tree about four metres away. Then I heard the *psh psh psh* sound behind me and looked over my shoulder. On the cottage roof, perched right at the edge, only an arm's length away, was a different jay. Its head was cocked to the side, one eye looking right at me.

MY FAMILY SLEPT IN the old cottage and everyone else in the new one. Greg's family often stayed down at the boathouse during the summer, but it was even less insulated than the old cottage and was freezing in spring and fall.

Before my brother had a family, Ben, Yeats, and I slept in the boathouse. We walked down the path at dusk and sat on the dock with our feet in the water and talked over our day while kicking our legs and splashing one another. And then, every morning, Yeats would jump out of bed and rush to the front windows. He was looking for birds, and most mornings he would spot something: a great blue heron, a pair of loons, a merganser with her parade of ducklings. Then we'd spend hours on the path leading from the boathouse to the old cottage. I let Yeats set the pace and it was *slow*. We looked at every mushroom, every clump of moss. We stroked the moss gently with one finger each. We tipped delicate lady's slippers up to look closely at the hidden parts of the flowers. We looked for daddy-long-legs. We watched slugs trail their slime across mushrooms. We watched snails inch up the path and sometimes we moved them off into the forest. We had nothing but time and we spent a lot of it immersed in nature, teaching one another what it meant to pay close attention to every little thing.

All those hours on the path. The qualities one needed for successful birdwatching were apparent in Yeats from the start.

"Mom," he'd say. "We don't have to rush."

As Yeats grew older, we stepped off the path and into the forest. We saw a thousand mushrooms, all shapes, sizes, colours.

I said, "Look, it's a trail of treasure." I pointed to a cluster of tiny yellow mushrooms followed by two giant white ones pushing their way up through the fallen pine needles.

"And look at these," Yeats said, sweeping his arm past a long line of reddish-brown and slightly slimy mushrooms that led to a large cluster of perfect white toadstools covered in red nubbles.

We followed the mushrooms to the end of the forest and when we stepped out into the clear, Yeats stopped me with a hand gesture. He'd spotted a merlin, a small grey falcon. It was sitting at the top of a dead tree at the crest of the hill. We stood perfectly still and watched, afraid we would startle it.

I remember a scudding cloud covering the sun, the breeze picking up, and I heard Yeats·sighing with pleasure next to me. Then I heard his sharp intake of breath when the bird left its perch and flew, circling, circling.

I didn't know, of course, that Yeats's early and insistent interest in birds would persist throughout his childhood and into his teens. I didn't know that I'd be driving hundreds of kilometres to see migrating warblers in southern Ontario or planning a trip to Tofino on Vancouver Island to paddle with the eagles.

We never know what kinds of trips our children will take us on, but one thing I've learned over these twenty years is to trust my son's instincts and to encourage his interests. I listened to him, he listened to me (mostly), and it wasn't a stretch to say that birding helped us to maintain the closeness we'd had since he was a little boy.

TWO

WE MOVED INTO OUR Riverdale house six weeks before Yeats was due. I was still officially the manager at Book City on Danforth Avenue, but for those last weeks I did my final round of buying from home. The publishers' representatives came to visit me and we sat in the sparsely furnished living room, chatting about books and babies, and then I hauled the catalogues two blocks to the shop.

The house had a tiny backyard surrounded by big trees, full of squirrels and raccoons. Full of birds. We'd always had a bird feeder, except when we became temporarily frustrated by wily squirrels.

We called our kitchen window "Cat TV" because we'd also always had a cat. Cat TV was where we (and the cat) sat to watch birds and squirrels and, sometimes, other cats. It was a good introduction to Toronto backyard birds: black-capped chickadees, blue jays, house sparrows and house finches, white-breasted nuthatches, northern cardinals, dark-eyed juncos. I grappled with the morality of having an outdoor cat because cats are hunters, but modern life is full of such contradictions and although I couldn't justify this one I also couldn't seem to rectify it. Pippin would have killed me if I didn't let him outside. It's a complicated world we live in and I allowed myself some comfort in the knowledge that our cat actually spent most of his life sound asleep on the third floor of the house.

I bought the house with money I had inherited from my father. It was semi-detached and one hundred years old. We didn't have much stuff when we moved in, which meant we had extra room for the children to play in, and over the years we created a warm, welcoming environment. A friend once said to me, "Your house is so serene. I always feel relaxed when I'm here." She looked around. "How do you do it?" She wasn't there when all the kids were! I'd grown up in a very quiet household and I remember visiting friends in their homes and envying them the busy ruckus and racket of older brothers or singing fathers. Now I had both of those worlds — a ruckus when all the children were with us (although Ben didn't do too much singing at any time), and quiet when it was just the three of us. I'd never lived in the same place for more than six years, and that was when I was a child. I moved into the house in Riverdale with the hope that we'd stay put and it would be as stable an environment as I could make it for the family. I was tired of moving and I was going to be a stay-at-home mom.

I had the quiet house to myself during the day, with Ben off to work and Yeats off to school. I took a studio art course for the first time in my life, which was fun but made me realize why I'd never gravitated in that direction. My talent was *very* limited. I joined a writing group, The Moving Pen, where I did belong. I was home for Yeats when he came back from school, when he was sick, when he needed me. I volunteered in the school library when Yeats was in elementary school and went on all the field trips. It was how I was raised and how Ben was raised, too, and it felt right to us, as difficult as it sometimes was for me to be home alone with a small child.

We tried various activities: gymnastics, swimming, skating, art classes, music. Yeats refused to consider joining a team sport even though most of his friends played hockey or soccer. I found this amusing since the only sport I ever played in school was tennis, which is hardly a team sport. The only activity Yeats wanted to do for more than one season was art, although he had to continue with swimming since we had a cottage on an island. Most of my friends' children were enrolled in something every day, or nearly every day. They had a healthy balance of sports, music, and art, but they had almost no time to themselves. Yeats had lots of time to play and to read books, something our entire family valued.

I felt some societal pressure to *make* Yeats engage in more activities but he stubbornly refused. Mom said, "Remember your brother? He refused to go to day camp when he was little. You and Laurie went merrily onto the school bus every morning, but I'd have to carry Greg out there. He'd be kicking and screaming and he'd thrust his arms and legs out and push them against the door jams of the bus. After a few days of that, I gave up and he stayed home." Given the chance, Yeats would have done the same.

The other thing that Yeats would have been happy to foreswear was school itself. Yeats went to Withrow Public School and then to Earl Grey for Grades 7 and 8, and now he was preparing for high school, which he dreaded. The lessons were relatively easy for him — that wasn't the issue. His problem, from his very first day, was that school took up too much time, time that could have been spent doing whatever it was he really wanted to do. I asked other mothers if it was the same with their kids. It turned out that most of my friends' children went quite willingly to school. Most of the girls *loved* school.

Kindergarten had been okay since it was only in the morning and we spent the rest of the day together, going to Riverdale Farm, visiting friends or Nanny, or just hanging out. But once he started Grade 1 and had homework on top of school, he began to rebel. Every morning it was the same thing.

"Why do I have to go to school?"

"To learn things. You're learning to read. You're learning French (all the kids were enrolled in French Immersion, at least in the early years). You're learning math."

"I can learn those things at home. You can teach me."

"You're also making friends. Everyone needs friends."

"I don't have any friends."

"Yes, you do. It's time to go. You're going to be late."

He struggled and argued and kicked up a fuss. He railed against the system. Homework was especially awful and he was sure to take two hours to do twenty minutes' worth of math, dropping his pencil fifty times on the kitchen floor. I would yell at him and tear at my hair. I threatened to take away his homework, which made him finish it right away. By the time he was in Grade 4 I realized that as much as Yeats hated the homework, he wanted to do a good job. It was important to him to do it well, but the cost was huge. The ongoing struggle that we experienced with homework mirrored a more general debate that was raging throughout the school system. No one seemed to be in agreement, pedagogically, as to whether homework was a good or bad thing for children. (From my own experience with Yeats, I would say bad.)

By the time Yeats finished Grade 8, he was sick of school and especially of homework. He said, "High school's going to be so hard, Mom. I won't be able to do it. They're going to expect way too much of us, and I'm going to have hours of homework every night and no time for anything else."

"Who told you this?" I asked. "You're a smart boy, Yeats. You'll be able to do the work, just as you always have."

"But the homework!"

"Does Danielle have reams of homework that she can't do? Did Rupert? No. Look at Danielle. She has lots of time for dance lessons and hanging out with her friends."

"Hmph. I just know it's going to be bad. I hate homework."

Over the summer, he slowly worked himself into a state. Nothing I said could convince him he was going to be fine.

IN THE FALL OF 2007, Yeats started high school. He chose to go to Jarvis Collegiate, from which Rupert had already graduated. Rupert decided not to go directly to university, but to work with Ben at Nicholas Hoare Books. Titus had graduated from high school years before and was doing an apprenticeship with a carpenter. Danielle was going into her final year at Jarvis, but other than her and some of her friends, Yeats knew no one at the school. He said that was partly why he chose it: to have a fresh start and meet some new people.

Sometime during the first weeks of September, Yeats came home from school elated. He wouldn't tell me about his day, just that it was "okay." I figured I'd find out sooner or later why he was so happy and by the end of the week, I had the story. It was Ben who told me.

He said, "I heard it from Danielle. She told me that she took Yeats to the first meeting of something called Art Beat."

"What's that?" I asked.

"It's the poetry club. It meets once a week after school and puts out a magazine called *Art Beat* a couple of times a year. They also put together a coffee house at the end of the year, for students and teachers to entertain one another."

"Danielle's joining the poetry club?" That surprised me. Poetry really wasn't Danielle's thing.

"No. She just took Yeats to the first meeting."

Danielle had taken her baby brother by the hand and led him to where he belonged, making it easy for Yeats to find a place for himself in high school. Her generosity made me weepy with gratitude. Danielle simply shrugged and said, "That's okay. It was nothing, really."

But it *was* something, because it made the transition to high school so much easier for her brother. It reminded me of the spring of 1997, when I'd made an appointment for us to visit Withrow, where Yeats would be starting junior kindergarten that September. He didn't want to go, so we hung out in the playground for a while. When he calmed down, I said, "Let's just go in and say hi to the teacher. Maybe you can play with the sand toys."

He looked at me and started to cry.

"I'm not leaving you here. We're just visiting."

"But you'll be leaving me here later, when I'm in kindergarten!" He began to wail.

We were late for our appointment and I was starting to feel exasperated, so I scooped him up and hauled him through the kindergarten entrance. I set him down and looked to my left, towards the Grade 1 lunchroom. Danielle was sitting at a table with some other girls. She saw us and waved. I said to Yeats, who was still crying, "Look! There's Danielle!" He looked up and his face made that transformation that only children are capable of—from utter despair to overwhelming joy in one split second. I silently blessed my stepdaughter. Yeats's love and trust of his sister was complete. Danielle has always been his number one star.

So the transition to high school went more smoothly than we'd anticipated, and for that I had Danielle partly to thank. But as time went on, as much as Yeats enjoyed Art Beat and a few of his classes, the old homework beast began to raise its ugly head. Some kids procrastinated by watching movies or playing video games or going on their social media. Of his own choosing, Yeats didn't partake of those activities, and we didn't have a television. Instead, he came downstairs and ranted and raved at me. It was exhausting and crazy-making and half the time, I'd shut his words out. There are only so many times a person can answer the question, "Why do we have to do homework?"

AT THE SAME TIME Yeats began high school, we opened Ben McNally Books on Bay Street in downtown Toronto. Ben had spent the last fourteen years managing Nicholas Hoare Books and was more than ready to have his own shop, be his own boss. He wanted a place spacious enough for book launches and stunning enough to one day be called "the most beautiful bookstore in Canada." It was Ben's dream shop, full of wooden bookshelves with artistic detailing, an open space with high ceilings and ornate chandeliers, but also quiet little spaces where a person could feel alone with the books.

Bay Street was the heart of Toronto's financial district and our store was just north of the cluster of the city's tallest towers. We were blocks away from the headquarters of all the major banks — the black buildings of the TD Centre, the golden towers of RBC gleaming like giant jewels in the sun — as well as hundreds of law firms, advertising agencies, and real estate offices. Just north of us were Toronto City Hall and Old City Hall, full of judges, civil servants, and bureaucrats, all, we hoped, looking for good books to read.

We spent a busy year designing and building the store until its grand opening in September, 2007. From January of that year, Ben had run an office from our basement at home. But he also spent hours in the store space, which was in an old downtown building that was once a bank. He met with the designer, the banker, the book publishers. He dealt with the problems with the ventilation and the plumbing. He met with the cabinetmaker who customized the gorgeous bookcases for us. He acquired his first-ever credit card — a sign of the apocalypse, according to one of Ben's oldest friends.

One day Ben came home and said, "I'm thinking of getting a cell phone." I stared at him. My mouth must have been hanging open because he said, "What? All these people need to get in touch with me all the time. Sometimes it's an emergency; I need to make a lot of decisions."

I said, "A cell phone? Is this Ben McNally?"

He blinked at me a couple of times and then laughed. "You're right. I'm not getting a cell phone."

The fact that Ben was even contemplating having a cell phone told me that big changes were afoot. Every so often he joked about getting a television, especially to watch the World Cup, but I knew he was just kidding around. The cell phone had sounded real, though. I remember thinking, *From this point on, our lives will be different.*

Ben asked me to help with the buying, but to do that I needed to work in the store to have a sense of the customers. I'd spent the past fourteen years at home with Yeats, and now I was dipping my toe back into the wider culture. I decided to work two days a week to start.

I'd begun my bookselling career in December, 1986. I was hired as a temporary clerk over the Christmas season in a tiny old Classics store on Bloor Street. I remember standing behind the cash register on my first day, looking over the shop and feeling a profound sense of belonging: *This is what I'm meant to be doing.* When that job ended after Christmas, I applied for a position at Book City on Yonge Street. Ben hired me, which was how we met, and he was my boss. So I guess we'd had some practice in these roles, however long ago it was.

Eventually, I became manager at the Book City on the Danforth. When I left to have the baby a customer said to me, "Don't quit work and jeopardize your career. Don't lose yourself." I guess that had happened to her, but my wage at Book City would have covered daycare and not much else, so I didn't even consider staying. Now that I was contemplating working again, the bookseller inside me was hopping with anticipation. I really did belong in a bookstore.

In the months leading up to the grand opening, I sometimes resented the near-constant companionship at home (which is crazy to think about now, when Ben works double shifts all week long and I almost never see him). I was used to having the house to myself and found sharing it with Ben an adjustment. Not that he was a disagreeable companion; just that he was there. I was reminded of my Uncle Dick who, on his first day of retirement, came downstairs to find a brown paper bag on the kitchen counter.

"What's this?" he asked my aunt.

"Your lunch," she said. "You're not hanging around the house all day."

By the summer, Ben had hired some staff, including Rupert and Danielle. We now had a basement office at the shop, which was fixed with desks and lots of metal shelving. The kids, along with a full-time employee, Lisa, started creating title cards on the computer system and receiving boxes of books. They had to unpack the boxes to make sure all the books were there, match the orders to the invoices, and pack the books up again until we could place them on the shelves upstairs. Upstairs was still under construction.

Over the Labour Day weekend, we engaged the help of family and friends to stock the shelves of the brand-new bookstore. It was very exciting for everyone. People picked their sections: our friend Mary chose to shelve kids' books; June and Johanna covered the biographies; Sarah and Fiona did hardcover fiction. Yeats and his friends started with the humour section and moved on to travel. Everywhere people were opening boxes, moving shelves around, and standing back to look at their handiwork. By the end of the weekend, we were exhausted but glowing with satisfaction. We were ready for business.

THAT FIRST FALL WE had two big parties in the store on back-to-back nights. We wanted to celebrate the grand opening of the shop with everyone we knew and we wanted to show our publishing friends that the store would be a good space for their parties. Eventually, we'd have not only book launches in the store, but weddings, showers, retirement parties, a play, even my mother's eightieth birthday party. The space began to take on a patina of worn charm.

But in the early days everything was new and shiny. People walked in and gawked at the beautiful chandeliers and bookcases, and every time I was there a customer would say something like, "This is a real sanctuary on Bay Street." "Bay Street" is synonymous with material wealth and success, but also with the rat race and with stress, something the shop's ambiance seemed to counteract. We had the feeling right, we had the book selection right, and now we just needed about a thousand more regular customers to make it a viable operation.

To that end, Ben started accepting every bookselling opportunity, be it holding an event in the store or hauling boxes of books to sell around town. We agreed to sell books for Random House at Word on the Street, the annual outdoor book festival that took place at Queen's Park at the end of September. This was where Yeats had his first taste of bookselling, and he loved it. He came with us to set up, piling books on the tables in the hopes of watching those stacks slowly shrink over the course of the day. He stayed all day without complaint and I remember thinking that it was in the blood, this bookselling, this willingness to stand around all day and talk about practically nothing but books.

Rupert worked in the store full-time for the first four years. Titus helped out at events for a while and then worked full-time in the store for about a year while he was between careers. Danielle worked in the store during the summers when she was home from university, and Yeats worked as many outside events as Ben would give him. It was a family business, and it didn't take long before publicists and editors got used to seeing us everywhere.

But it was a big change for the family. Ben was working long hours and it was a whole new schedule for me. I said that if I didn't work in the shop, I'd never see my husband. I said it as if it was a joke, but it was true.

"And how is that?" people asked. "How is it having your husband as your boss?"

"I compartmentalize," I said. "He's my boss at work and I'm the boss at home."

The truth was a bit more complicated, however. I tried not to step on Ben's toes but sometimes I just couldn't help but stick my nose into the running of the store. One of my pet peeves was the lighting. The ceiling was so high in the shop that we needed a 15-foot ladder to change the bulbs. The building maintenance guys did this for us but only when they had the time, since it wasn't really in their job description. Sometimes fifteen or more light bulbs would be out around the shop and it drove me crazy. It was dark in the corners and a lot of our customers were older than me. If I was having trouble seeing things, they sure would be. Would you buy a book you couldn't see?

I got on Ben's case about the bulbs. I asked him every time I was in if he'd called Scott. He reminded me that Scott couldn't just come; he had to wait until there were two of them with nothing else to do. Someone had to hold the ladder. Then another couple of bulbs went out and I nearly lost my mind. I had to bite my tongue or risk having Ben lose his temper. Would he really do that? When was the last time he really lost his temper at me? I couldn't remember, but I didn't want to risk it.

The light bulbs were just one example. Staffing was another. We had four full-time staff in the beginning: Rupert, Lisa, Rachna, and Simone. Over the years we lost Lisa and Rachna, and then Rupert. Ben didn't replace any of them. Business wasn't as busy as we would have liked, but there were times when we needed more staff in the shop. By the time we had consistently hectic days, we were chronically short-staffed. Ben was often the only person there in the morning, which meant he couldn't catch up on his administrative business. The way he saw it, though, he was saving money on wages.

I wasn't the boss. I tried not to interfere, but sometimes I walked a fine line. If he was in a good mood while I was razzing him, Ben would cock an eyebrow at me and say, "Really?" If he was pissed off for some reason, or just exhausted, he'd say, "Yes, dear." That was my cue to shut up. He never used the word "dear" as an endearment.

If Ben was particularly annoyed about something, a shipping or billing problem for example, I'd say to Simone, "Don't worry. I'll make sure we fool around tonight and he'll be better tomorrow." She'd groan and say, "Too much information." Or we'd wait until Ben was in the office downstairs and we'd go on a clearing spree behind the cash. (Ben never threw anything out.) Simone and I developed all kinds of eye signals and facial expressions to help one another get through Ben's moods. Actually, Ben wasn't really a moody man, but he was full of colourful expressions and sudden bursts of disapproval and frustration. During those fourteen years at home, I hadn't seen much of this side of him, so I told myself I'd have to find a way to navigate around his humours.

This was a whole new episode in our lives together, and it did take a bit of figuring out. I can't count the number of times I bit my tongue, especially in that first year when we were sorting out how to work together. Most of the time, though, working in the shop was a pure joy. I loved hand-selling books to customers, talking about the titles I especially loved with whoever was around, making displays. Even the really slow days in the shop were a pleasure for me. By the time I arrived home at the end of a day, spent on my feet, I felt like I'd earned my wage.

Most weeks I worked two shifts, but as time went on I began to work more events and at Christmas I took on more shifts, too. I started to let some things slide at the house — my standard of tidiness took a nose-dive until I couldn't stand it anymore and went on a cleaning frenzy. Little projects, such as clearing old toys or clothes out of boxes in the basement, were wiped right off the to-do list.

Ben worked much longer hours than he had at Nicholas Hoare, because of all our after-hours events. Yeats sometimes stayed late at school. It was harder to find time for everyone to be together, and I was starting to become concerned about Ben's health. His feet were sore all the time. His knees were sore, too, and he didn't eat properly. He'd forgo breakfast and lunch, eat a donut or maybe a croissant part way through the day, and then gorge on whatever we had in the kitchen when he arrived home at 10 p.m. My role as keeper of the household was slipping, which wasn't all bad. Yeats, for example, needed more independence. I loved these guys, though, and wanted us to keep our customary closeness, not drift apart because of day-to-day busy-ness.

THREE

THOSE FIRST FEW MONTHS after the opening of Ben McNally Books were tumultuous for me and for the family. Ben was always tired, always working. We had many firsts of what would become regular events: the first televised announcement of the Governor General's Literary Awards, the first Word on the Street, the first International Festival of Authors, our first crazy Christmas season, and plenty of book launches in between.

I hadn't wanted us to be the official bookseller at the IFOA, which is the International Festival of Authors held at Harbourfront in Toronto each October. It felt too soon to me to open the store in September and then have to set up a second shop somewhere else, moving all those books in and out and staffing the ten-day event. But Ben's mind was made up.

"If we turn it down this year, we might not get a second chance," he said.

Ben loved the festival: being in the thick of things with authors and publishers from around the world, going to all the late-night parties. That first year, I worked more hours in our actual bookshop, and by the time I got home I was too tired to go to many of the parties. I wasn't used to this type of work — being on my feet for eight hours and dealing with other people's energy all day long. Our customers were far from rude or obnoxious, but they were people who required my attention and I couldn't just go lie down on the couch for fifteen minutes to recharge.

When I had first started working with Ben at Book City all those years ago, we didn't have a computer system. We used small cards, like flashcards, to keep inventory, and we phoned our orders in to the publishers. We knew every book in the store because we were in such close contact with them all the time. I loved moving through that old store, looking for all the, say, books published by Ballantine, ordering the ones that were popular and pulling older stock off the shelves. It was unhurried work and I was good at it.

At the new store, we had a computerized inventory system as well as the Internet. All our buying was done on the computer. Every once in a while we had to check the shelves to see if we really did have that one copy of the book the computer said we had, but most often we didn't. At first I resented the computer. I wanted to gather up a fistful of cards and go count the books. I was afraid that I'd come to rely too much on the machine and had forgotten all my specialized knowledge. But I learned to satisfy my love of handling the books by making displays and spending time each day browsing the shelves.

I adjusted. I adjusted to working outside the home and to using the computer, and I began to adapt to Ben's newfound workaholism. Yeats worked weekends with us at the IFOA and at our monthly author brunches. But he was also adjusting to high school—finding his way in a new environment, just as I was.

IN MID-NOVEMBER BEN AND I took a taxi together from the shop up to Jarvis for our parent-teacher interviews. Yeats liked most of his Grade 9 teachers. He found it amazing that they talked to the students as if they were adults who could make their own choices about how to run or ruin their lives.

The teachers liked Yeats, too. He was one of the boys who listened. I was reminded of his Grade 3 gym teacher, who'd been new to Withrow. She approached me in the yard one day and said, "You're Yeats's mom, aren't you?" When I said yes, she said, "I just want you to know that he's one of only two boys who actually listen to what I say. You can be proud of him."

Six years later, he was still listening. He didn't have that restlessness many boys experience, partly because he was so good at paying attention.

One of his Grade 9 teachers said, "Yeats is one of those

students you can't rush. He needs assignments that allow him to go deep into something, not just skim the surface."

I couldn't believe that someone understood Yeats this quickly—in less than two months.

"He's one of those students who's making connections between things everywhere he goes," he said, "but that kind of thinking takes time. He'll get frustrated if people try to rush him."

When we got home later that night, I told Yeats about that conversation.

He just shrugged. "That won't stop them from making me do all the dumb little assignments. You'll see."

Of course he was right. But at least he knew that some of the teachers appreciated who he was. The teachers saw the calm, attentive Yeats, the Yeats who could deal with the pressures of school. In class, Yeats was unfailingly cheerful and helpful. He participated in discussions and did well on his tests and assignments. He wasn't one of those kids who took his angst out on the world. (He saved that for me!)

Since the start of high school Yeats had decided to do his homework on his own in his room. We had made a pact. I wouldn't ask him one thing about his homework, ever, and he'd do it without coercion. Mostly I was able to hold up my side of the bargain. Sometimes I forgot.

"How was school?" I'd say.

He'd grunt.

I'd say, "Did you do your presentation? How did it go?"

"Fine."

"Did your teacher like the music you chose?"

"Mom, I don't want to talk about it."

In an act of desperation or insanity I'd completely forget my promise and say, "Do you have homework for tonight?"

"Mom! I can't believe it! Stop asking me that! Just stop!" As though I'd been asking for ages when it had really been weeks since the last lapse. He'd stomp upstairs, heaving great sighs, slam his bedroom door, and play something loud on his stereo. At least I loved all his music.

For some reason, one night he chose to do his homework at the kitchen table. My big mistake was not telling him to do the work in his room, but I guess I was happy to have the company while I prepared dinner.

As he worked at his math, he became physically agitated first, then vocally, and then asked for my help, which I was unable to supply since my math skills no longer went beyond Grade 8. He ranted a bit about math in general, then about school, and the longer he went on the more my blood boiled. *If he spent half as much time on the actual work as he did on complaining about it . . .*

My first response, which with tremendous effort I kept to myself, was to turn into a fire-breathing dragon and burn down the whole house with us in it. Instead, I threw down my paring knife and said, "I don't need to listen to this. I don't need to be part of this," and then I stomped upstairs.

I felt like a failure because I'd risen instantly to such strong emotion, but I also felt touched by grace because I'd let it go almost as quickly. I sat on my bed and breathed for a few minutes, listening to him scratch away with his pencil, doing the work. I closed my eyes and asked for wisdom: how to help Yeats get through high school, how to balance what he needed from me with everything else I needed to do in my life. Why was it, I wondered, that my parents had known practically nothing about what my siblings and I were doing in school, while these days, everyone I knew was involved in their children's education? I couldn't work out if this was a good thing or not.

When I went upstairs later in the evening, Yeats called to me from his bedroom. I went in and sat on his chair.

He said, "Why do I have to do well at school? Why can't I just enjoy myself and do okay, but maybe not really well?"

We'd been over this territory a thousand times since Grade 1, but learning is a process of repetition, if nothing else.

"Two things. One, it's far more satisfying in the long term to do something well, to do the best you can. To know in your heart that you did all you could. It's a personal reward. The other reason is more practical—so you can get into the university of your choice."

Big sigh from the big boy. "But what if I don't want to go to university?"

"Then you'll work instead, or travel for a bit and then go to university, or volunteer somewhere and work part-time." He knew all of this, but he needed to hear it again. And again.

"I guess I'll go to university. But I'm not interested in anything. I don't know what to take. I'm not good at anything."

"Yeats, you're interested in everything!" It infuriated

me when he said stuff like this. He thought his teachers were crazy to give him high marks. Certainly nothing I could say would reassure him so I just said, "When the time comes, we'll go over the course offerings together and see what appeals to you. You don't have to decide on a major going in to first year."

"Hmph."

I was tired of this conversation but I knew it was important. It wasn't that I didn't care, just that I wished he'd have more faith in himself.

"But high school, Mom. They're always trying to make everybody into the same person. It was the same when we were younger, too. All school is like that, I guess."

"That's not true," I said. "Those teachers appreciate who you are, care about you as an individual."

"Maybe some teachers. But, I mean, the system as a whole. They want us all to behave in the same way and we're all supposed to go on to university and make something big of ourselves. What if we don't want that? There's so much pressure," he said.

As I sat with Yeats, I thought about him on a kindergarten field day, just before he turned five. The boys were lined up to run a race, the teacher counting down from three, and off they went, running across the grass as fast as their little legs would take them.

Halfway down the field Yeats stopped and crouched. He'd spotted something and took his time looking at it, gently tipping up whatever it was with one finger.

The teacher yelled, "Yeats! Keep running!"

He looked up at her, then at all the parents who were laughing on the sidelines, then at his classmates who were already at the finish line. He stood up and ran to the end of the field and then came over to me.

"What was it?" I asked. "What did you see?"

"A really pretty flower, Mom. A tiny blue flower, in the grass." This was his true nature. Not one iota of competitiveness. He could care less about the race.

Then I remembered when Laurie, Greg, and I were teens, and how Dad used to ask us at night, "Did you win today?" This question always made me want to explode, but we weren't allowed to get angry so I just sulked and scowled and told him I didn't know what he meant since I wasn't in a competition. Of course I knew what he meant, but I didn't like this implication that there was winning and losing and nothing else. Dad came from a family with huge expectations and he raised us in the same way. I remember him asking my brother Greg, when he'd made 98 percent on a math test, what had happened to the other 2 percent. He also regularly asked, "Where do you see yourself ten years from now?" I hated that question too. I tried to convince him that knowing where I was right *now* was far more important. He didn't buy it. I was loath to impose that level of expectation on my son, because I remembered so clearly how I'd reacted as a child. But I was conflicted. On the one hand, aiming for success had been bred into me; on the other, my measure of success was quite different from my father's. As a parent, it made me ask myself: Is it a blessing or a curse to be in this world without worldly ambition, without the drive to win and accumulate?

When we were finishing high school, Dad's definition of success became more concrete — success meant a respectable, prosperous career. Laurie wanted to study physics at university, but Dad told her she'd wind up working for the government in a dead-end laboratory job. Dad, a star hockey player in high school, had been drafted to play in a professional Ontario league. His mother had said no, there wasn't enough money in hockey. Then he wanted to study medicine, but his father said no, business was a better option. Now he told his daughter that she should study economics, instead of following her passion, so she did.

And I remember, too, the day Greg called from university, where he was in second-year engineering. Dad had done an engineering degree before going on to business school, and it seemed this was Greg's path, too. But Greg was bored to death by engineering and had decided to switch to economics (which sounded dreadfully boring to me).

I answered the phone and Greg told me why he was calling. He said, "Dad won't understand. He's going to be really mad."

He was nervous, but I pointed out that I'd done way worse than that. "Don't you remember, Greg? I took a whole year off university, between second and third year. I went travelling, for God's sake! Then I switched universities. You're just switching programs."

"Was Dad mad at you?"

"Maybe. I don't know. Do what you have to do."

Laurie and Greg both went on to get MBAS, while I had my more or less useless undergrad degree in history. But I remember one day Dad said to me, "You're just about the only kid I know with a real university education." I took that as a compliment, and then I watched my brother and sister take jobs with management-consulting firms and proceed to work themselves to the bone. Within a few years, both of them ended up leaving that business, questioning the path that had led them there.

I, on the other hand, had no path at all. I just went with whatever seemed to come up. It was how I'd always lived and how Ben lived, too, and it informed how we raised the children.

We all live with unintended consequences, and maybe we should have been pushing Yeats, and our other kids, to be more productive during their growing years, so they'd have more to show for themselves on their resumes. Maybe working for their bookselling parents just wasn't enough to give them a taste of the world and all its trials. The real world. But then we would have been untrue to our ourselves.

Some days I agonized over this. But I reminded myself it was good to challenge people's notions of how to live, and this was something that Yeats had been doing, naturally and quietly, since he was born.

AFTER A QUIET NEW year and a busy spring, we went up to
the cottage. We arrived at the lake and stood on the dock at
the golf club. We'd called ahead, so Greg and his little boys
would be coming in a boat to pick us up, but for these few
minutes we stood and breathed Muskoka in.

Ben said, "It's nice here," as we watched a couple of cormorants fly past, low to the water. He put his arm around me.
"Thanks, Lynn." I nodded, made speechless once again by
the familiar beauty of the lake, the view of islands and boathouses and dark blue water.

It was the May 24th long weekend—time to officially
open the family cottage for another season. We came north
with the birds, during their yearly migration. We stocked
up on staples: baking goods, oils and spices, bags of dried
beans, rice, raisins, coffee. We had a bag of books to read,
too, although we knew we had hours of chores ahead of us.
It was the same every year and something in that sameness
comforted me, made me feel rooted in that landscape.

Our first weekend of the season was always a busy one.
We moved the deck furniture out from the screened-in porch
and replaced it with the white wicker furniture from the main
bedroom. We got the dock furniture from the boathouse and
the floaty-toys down from one of the boathouse bedrooms.
We cleaned the eavestroughs at the new cottage and swept
pine needles off the roof of the old cottage. Pine needles are
very acidic and will eventually rot the shingles.

Someone had bought bedding plants, and we all worked
together in the garden. Planting had taken most of a day when

the children were small, but now that they were old enough to help it took only a couple of hours.

Every year, though, something was amiss. Perhaps it would be a broken water pipe under the old cottage, or the dishwasher leaking all over the kitchen floor because it hadn't been properly hooked up. Perhaps the chimney flashing would have come loose, rainwater making its way through the roof, or an animal would have ripped holes in the screens. This year, it was a nest of dead mice in an old coffee pot.

At the end of the day we had a big family dinner. Everyone crowded around the table, which was full of bottles of wine and Ben's fresh bread, candles burning and Van Morrison on the stereo. That first weekend together was always joyful for me and, I think, for the entire family. Muskoka was our cherished place, a never-changing refuge from our everyday lives.

From the time we first bought the island, when Laurie was still living in England, my siblings and I had counted on the lake to bring us together. We spent hours on the dock, talking, swimming, and teaching various little children how to dive and waterski.

We took the kids to the small beach on the west side of the island, and Ben spent hours there finding rocks to build a breakwater so we'd lose less sand from the beach. We sat on what we called Family Rock, a rock big enough for two adults and two or three small children to sit on, squished together. Over the years, Laurie and I spent hour upon hour sitting on Family Rock, watching the kids swim and build sandcastles, securing our sisterhood.

While Greg and his young family spent most weekends at the cottage, we were too busy to do that. After we opened the cottage, we returned to the city and to our busy lives. We had to wait until the summer to take full advantage of our family oasis.

THE STORE WAS QUIET that first summer, as it has been every summer since. The financial district emptied out; everyone was travelling to cottages and camps, taking overseas holidays or just enjoying time off at home. Our staff took vacation time, too, so they weren't milling around the store with no customers to serve. Ben took his customary two weeks off at the beginning of July. While he flopped on a chaise and read all day, I bugged him to take more time off, later in the summer.

"Maybe," he said.

The days grew hot and we spent time in the forest and time on the lake. Ben called work every day and if there was a problem (which there almost never was), he managed it from afar.

I said, "Why don't you give them a day off from hearing from you? Let them know they can manage on their own."

"Why would I do that?" he asked.

"So they know you trust them to run the place."

"Do I?"

"You should. It would be good for you, too. To stop thinking about it so much."

"If I didn't call, I'd be thinking about it even more."

I stared at him, wondering how it was he didn't understand what I was trying to say. Maybe I was the one not understanding.

"But they'll call you," I said, "if there's something wrong."

"Maybe."

I gave up and went for a kayak instead. I knew that once summer was over and we were back in the city, our lives would diverge again. Ben's weeks would fill up with events: Monday night selling books at a reading, Tuesday at a launch in the store, Wednesday down at Harbourfront, Thursday another launch in the store. If we were lucky, he'd have Friday and Saturday nights off, although as time went on, that was never a given. He'd started selling books in Kensington Market a few Sundays a year, and we had our own Sunday brunch series as well as author dinners at Grano, an Italian restaurant on Yonge Street. Taken singly, these events were great fun and sometimes even edifying, but the pace was relentless.

I decided that even if Ben didn't want to take a holiday far from the store that summer, I needed to. I booked Yeats and me a trip to British Columbia, to spend some time on Vancouver Island visiting friends and driving out to Tofino on the west side of the island. I'd heard about Tofino since I'd lived in BC in my twenties, and I longed to see it for myself—its beaches, the endless ocean, the forests.

I asked Ben to join us but he said, "No thanks." He smiled at me. "I like my holidays at the cottage where I can read a stack of books."

I liked that kind of holiday, too, but it was nice to mix things up. It was nice to go somewhere new.

FOUR

YEATS AND I TRAVELLED to Vancouver by train. He was fifteen. He brought along his portable CD player but didn't use it once during the four days and three nights we were on the train. We sat in the observation car, mesmerized by the scenery. First came Ontario, with its endless lakes and trees, deciduous followed by mixed forests. The train stopped in Parry Sound, on Georgian Bay, and travelled over the trestle bridge. It was the longest bridge in Ontario, standing high over the water.

As the train turned west past Lake Superior, the mixed forests gave way to mostly evergreens. Yeats said, "Ontario goes on forever! Forest after forest, lake after lake. Did you know it was this big?"

"Yes. Nanny took the three of us on the train to Winnipeg

the year I was fourteen, remember?"

"Oh, yeah. You told me."

"It seems to me we spent most of the time playing cards, or sitting in the dining car. The porter would come through the cars yelling, 'First call for dinner! Dining car forward!' and we'd follow behind, calling it out, too. Dad met us in Winnipeg and we drove west from there."

"So you only had one night on the train?"

"I guess so, but it looms large in my memory, maybe because we were moving from Toronto to Vancouver. It wasn't exactly a vacation — I was leaving my friends behind and going west to the unknown. Being on the train was fun, but it was bittersweet." I was guessing this trip would loom even larger for Yeats when he was grown, especially since it wouldn't be tinged with sadness as my trip had been. It would be four days of enforced relaxation.

I loved to travel and had done a lot of it — to Europe and Southeast Asia, to Africa and India. I loved the anticipation of travelling somewhere new, of being on the road. I'd had all kinds of good and bad experiences while travelling — from a transcendental moment at a tiny shrine in Darjeeling to contracting malaria in Zaire — and I'd intended to keep travelling after Yeats was born.

Ben was not a traveller. When the kids were small we took two family holidays to Florida. Ben came with us twice to visit Laurie and Andy in London, but he didn't come when Yeats and I went to see them in Greenwich. He didn't join us when Laurie and Andy took us on a holiday to Italy and he did not want to go to BC. He said, "I might like it there too much and want to stay."

He was only half joking. He said he didn't need to go anywhere new; that he was comfortable at the cottage and wouldn't get to read much anywhere else. Secretly, I thought it was his feet. He was afraid that if we went somewhere like Italy, he'd have to do a lot of walking and his feet would give out.

At first I wondered if I could bear to be married to someone who didn't care to travel, but I found ways around that. I took Yeats to places where I had friends to visit or we travelled with Laurie or Mom or sometimes both. I hoped that one day Ben would come with us.

As the train moved northward, we saw so many bald eagles that Yeats stopped bothering to count them after a while. We stopped in the rocky Canadian Shield at a tiny spot called Capreol and we had the porter, Charlie, take our photo there, with the train as backdrop. Not long after, the train stopped in the middle of nowhere and a family disembarked. Charlie helped a man, a woman, and two very small children off the train. The adults heaved huge packs and the four of them disappeared down a forest path that I swear opened up only as they walked down it. Charlie said these people had a cabin on the lake; they'd be waiting for the train on the southbound side in exactly one month's time, he told us.

In the week before our departure, there'd been an accident on the rails east of Toronto, and the freight trains all the way west were still backed up as a result. Our train stopped often, standing still for up to half an hour on the sidings, letting these freight trains roll by. We counted the cars as they passed. One train had more than 140 cars and by the time it had gone by, we were thoroughly and pleasantly transfixed.

Because of these delays, our train stopped for only half an hour in Winnipeg instead of a couple of hours. It was midnight and we stood on the street outside the station, looking one way and then the other. My father grew up in Winnipeg and maybe one night he'd stood in that very spot, looking up and down the street. Maybe when he, too, was fifteen.

We woke before sunrise and I crawled down from my windowless berth and joined Yeats in the one below. We watched the sun come up over the prairies, enthralled again by the sweep of colour, the endlessness of the Canadian landscape.

We stopped briefly in Saskatoon. I was already seated for breakfast but hadn't yet poured my coffee. I saw Yeats out on the platform and then suddenly he was at the table, saying, "Mom, you have to come outside. You have to smell this place." The two other people at my table laughed, but they came out, too.

We walked up and down the station platform, dizzy with the smells of the prairie, the grasses, the freshness. This was *air*.

My grandmother, Mary (who we called Mort), grew up on a farm near Arcola, Saskatchewan, and I thought of her and how strong she always seemed, how centred. I wondered how much Mort missed her old home once she moved to the city. I remembered her telling us about riding a horse to school and about her brother, Tom, who was killed as a young man when the tractor he was trying to repair rolled onto his neck.

There was a photo of Mary and Tom taken when they were in their twenties. It was a close-up in black and white, and the first time I saw it I was stunned by my grandmother's beauty. I knew her only as an older woman, but here she was in her youth: high cheekbones, wavy, short blonde hair, clear and steady eyes. She was leaning on her brother's shoulder and smiling. He was tipping back his hat and grinning, too, his blond hair hidden. Mort kept that photo in her bathroom, where she would see it many times a day.

I remembered visiting the farm in Arcola on that journey west when I was fourteen, drinking fresh lemonade in the big open kitchen with all my cousins. Dad and his brother had spent a month every summer on that farm, doing chores and other farm work, and he loved it there. He wanted us to have a sense of that place, too.

Yeats and I had another truncated stop, this time in Jasper. Coming into town, our train had had to wait in a siding for over an hour; but it was far from boring. A black bear had come along and foraged for grain on the tracks directly behind the train. We were in the last car, and the porter removed the window from the rear door so we'd have a clear view of the bear. Every so often it would raise its head and sniff in our direction, but then it would go back to its task. It was exciting, but sad, too. We learned that bears often came to scrounge for wheat and other grain that fell through the cracks of freight cars; many of them were killed by trains that didn't see them until it was too late.

As we pulled into Jasper station, we saw a double rainbow out the back of the train and decided we'd been blessed. Because of all the delays, we'd be travelling through the Rockies at night, but this meant our next sunrise would be in the Thompson River Valley.

As we rode through the valley the next morning, Yeats said, "I didn't know we had a desert in Canada." The landscape was beautiful and sparse: orange-brown dunes rising from sage-dotted riverbanks, pine trees scanty on the hillsides. Yeats was right: it looked desert-dry. I wanted the train to stop so we could feel and smell the air there.

Our porter said to Yeats, "You are one lucky fifteen-year-old. Just wait till you tell your friends you took the train all the way from Toronto to Vancouver with your mother. They are going to be so envious!"

We stopped next in Kamloops, then had a slow ride into downtown Vancouver. For a while, the train stood unmoving on the south side of the Fraser River, among freight trains and loading zones. It was a clear day and we could see the North Shore mountains in the distance, with their dusting of snow on top. My heart constricted at this view: it was a reminder of the city I loved so much, and I was happy to be able to share it with my son, if not with my husband.

WE SPENT A COUPLE of days in Vancouver and then took the ferry from Horseshoe Bay to Nanaimo. Yeats and I stood out on deck and I took a photo of him with Mount Baker faintly visible in the background. It was a glorious day but windy and I decided to sit inside.

Yeats came with me so he'd know where I was sitting, and then he went back out on deck. He stood at the front of the ferry, by himself in the wind and sun, and danced. He wasn't shaking and twisting, but he was definitely dancing to a tune in his head. All of us seated in the big passenger area could see this lone boy, a tall fifteen-year-old with long, blond hair. He was bopping away, looking out to sea. His hair was flying, his hands were playing drums on the railing in front of him, and we were all watching.

I was feeling a bit shy for him. Well, I was shy but he wasn't, so what I was feeling was complicated. I didn't want him to stop dancing, but I wondered if he was distracting people from their view. Probably his happiness was contagious rather than irritating.

There is a point in that ferry ride when you can look back at the Coast Mountain range north of Vancouver and that's the point, every time, when I have my little breakdown. My throat tightens, my eyes tear up, and I swear to myself that one day, some day, I'll move back to the West Coast.

My family lived in Vancouver for two years starting when I was six and then again for one year when I was fourteen. At twenty-one, after my second year at Queen's University in Kingston, I moved back there for what was supposed to be a summer; I ended up staying for four years. That first summer it rained for more than forty consecutive days, but it didn't bother me. I was working at a company that packaged and distributed incense from a loft in an old industrial building in Gastown. My officemate taught people how to grow food in city spaces and he practised tai chi with his girlfriend at lunchtime. I was living my hippie dream, wearing long, flowing skirts and sharing a house with six other young people. When I called my parents to tell them I'd decided to take a year off school to work and then travel to India with my boyfriend, they were speechless. This was totally off-script, but they couldn't stop me.

I used to go with friends every summer to the Vancouver Folk Music Festival, held at Jericho Beach in Kitsilano. We'd buy a weekend pass and see as much live music as we could. I saw Rita MacNeil, Stephen Fearing, Roy Forbes (better known to us folkies as "Bim"), various Bulgarian wedding bands, and countless local musicians. One memorable night we left the park with the haunting repetition of Sweet Honey in the Rock singing "U.S. out of El Salvador" over and over and over. I remember turning my back on a little stage one day, looking out over the beach and English Bay, over to the mountains on the North Shore. This view, along with the feeling of deep well-being I had throughout the music festival, imprinted itself on my brain, so that whenever I heard the word "Vancouver" these memories came to mind.

When we reached that spot in the ferry ride, I went over

to the window to look at the mountains so I could torture myself. Then Yeats was beside me.

"Are you okay, Mom?"

"Yes. Why?"

"You look like you're crying."

"Just with happiness. It's so beautiful."

He cocked his head at me.

"What's up?" I said.

"Can I have some money for cookies?"

I gave him some change and he headed for the canteen. The woman next to me said, "Is that your son?"

"Yes."

She nodded and smiled, and said, "He looks like he's enjoying himself."

I noticed lots of people looking at me as Yeats regained the railing and resumed his dance. Yes, I am his mother.

MY FRIEND HEATHER, HER husband, Gord, and their teenaged daughter, Elizabeth, picked us up at the ferry. We drove down the island to a marina where they docked their boat. Their cabin was on De Courcy Island, a gulf island just south of Gabriola. De Courcy is a long, narrow island, about 300 acres of mostly forested land. There are about forty homes on the island, the majority of them seasonal, like our cottage in Muskoka. The boat trip to De Courcy wasn't long, about ten minutes, then another five or ten minutes in my friends' pickup truck to the cabin.

And it really was a cabin, perched on a small hillside above a rocky beach. It had a cozy living room/kitchen area and two small bedrooms. The fridge, stove, and on-demand hot water heater were all propane, and the lights and water pump worked off the solar panel installed on the lawn outside. They had a generator for backup, but we didn't need to run it while we were there.

There was a window seat that looked out over the water and a couch with armchairs around a pot-bellied stove. A long, wooden dining table sat alongside a row of floor-to-ceiling windows, and everything was within arm's reach of everything else.

We loved it. It was so vastly different from the cottage in Muskoka that I was instantly jealous.

Yeats said, "Why can't our cottage be like this?"

Heather laughed and said, "But I love your place in Muskoka! Wanna trade?"

Yeats thought about that but didn't say anything. Then he went outside to play badminton with Elizabeth, followed by their dog, Jake. Jake was a Maltipoo, the cutest and happiest dog I'd ever met.

Heather made a couple of gin and tonics, which we took out to a rocky point. For a split second I thought, *She's living my dream*. Then I let that go, not wanting to wallow in envy as we watched the sun go down into the ocean. Heather and I had been friends since we were eighteen, and I didn't begrudge her seemingly paradisiacal life. I was grateful to be there.

"The kids are trying to play badminton." Heather laughed. "It's far too windy."

"Jake wants to play, too," I said, watching the dog run from Elizabeth to Yeats and back again. "They're going to play with him instead." The kids put down the rackets and Elizabeth picked up a stick to throw.

"What are you guys going to do in Tofino? Take surfing lessons?" Heather laughed again. She knew we wouldn't be doing that.

"No. Whale-watching. Hiking. Maybe we'll go bird-watching."

"That'd be good. The last time we were there we went whale-watching and saw a whole pod of humpbacks. It was spectacular. I didn't even get seasick in the boat."

"I guess you'll never move back to Ontario?"

"Are you kidding me? Not in a million years. This coast is home. When we were away sailing in the Caribbean, Elizabeth was homesick for the cool weather. She really missed the rain and fog and everything else. I guess I did, too. You know, big cedars and stuff."

"Giant slugs."

"And the eagles."

"Don't they have eagle-like birds in the Caribbean?"

"It's not the same. These are our eagles. Don't you feel the same way about where you live?"

"Muskoka, yes. Toronto, not as much. But I'd really miss Muskoka if I moved back here. I know I would. I'd probably die of it, somewhere inside. One of those little deaths that add up, day by day, into something unbearable. The rocks, the lake, the pines. Yeah, you're right, I feel the same way."

We had five glorious days on De Courcy—hiking, swimming (I borrowed a wetsuit but Yeats went into the freezing Pacific without), boating, visiting Heather and Gord's friends, eating and talking. This particular cloud nine came to a gentle end back at the marina, where Alex, another Vancouver Island friend, picked us up. She took us to her house in Nanaimo, a small city on the east coast of the island.

Alex and I had met when she worked at a children's theatre company in Vancouver in the early 1980s and I took a summer job there helping the business manager, Susan. Susan was also still a friend, but she lived in Calgary now.

Alex's daughter, Breanna, was Danielle's age. She was at home for the summer, working in the restaurant of a retirement home. She stood in the kitchen and ate a large tub of yogurt in one go.

She said, "Momma, let's take them to Goats on Roof. I could get the day after tomorrow off."

"Great idea, darlin'!" Alex said. "You guys will love Goats on Roof."

"What is it?" Yeats asked.

Breanna said, "It's a market with a grassy roof with goats on it, grazing. The market is really great and they have all these beautiful hanging decorations inside. They look like lanterns, but they're not, just decorations. And they have every colour, some with little pieces of mirror in them. You'll love them."

Alex said, "You can buy them. They also have really yummy things to eat there, and lots of little shops selling groovy T-shirts and jewellery and things. It's a fun place to wander, to window-shop."

Yeats wasn't big on shopping but he nodded. In fact, Yeats hated shopping, but he was too polite to protest out loud.

Goats on Roof was at Coombs, which is just north of Nanaimo. The market was built in the 1970s by a couple who had immigrated to Canada from Norway. They used a traditional Norwegian construction style, building the market right into a slope and putting sod on the roof for insulation. Once it was built, they thought, *I wonder what would happen if we put goats on the roof to eat all this grass?* What happened was, it turned into a huge tourist attraction. The goats grazed happily and the market was fantastic, offering high quality food, kitchenware, and toys.

We ended up buying one of those colourful hanging decorations for each of Yeats's cousins, plus a couple for ourselves. I'd have liked to fill a whole room with them, hang them from every possible nook and cranny, and pretend I lived inside a hippie-nomad tent.

Alex and I spent some good time visiting while Yeats worked on their computer in the basement. He was putting together a collage of photos from the train trip.

The topic of home came up with this old friend, too. She asked if I'd ever move back to the coast. I shook my head.

"I don't think so anymore. I think I'm settled in the Canadian Shield," I said.

When I left Vancouver in 1985, I thought I'd go back. I thought I was returning to Ontario temporarily; but then I met Ben and we had Yeats. Although I wouldn't have called myself stuck in Toronto, whenever I travelled back to BC, I was reminded that it, too, was home.

"Oh, that's too bad. I want you out here. Ron wants to move somewhere even smaller than Nanaimo. Maybe Powell River." Ron was Alex's partner.

"What about you?" I asked her.

"If I move from Nanaimo, I think I'd like to go back to Vancouver. Breanna will be going to school there, probably UBC. But I don't think I'll be leaving here. I'm so settled. The thought of moving somewhere even quieter than here…"

"Remember we used to talk about when we're old? Really old. And a group of us women moving into a house together and looking after one another, once all our men are gone?" We laughed.

"Here, on the West Coast," Alex reminded me.

"Right. Well, I guess I can't count that out completely. It might still be in my future."

"I'll hold on to that thought, sweetie."

THE NEXT DAY ALEX dropped us off at the rental car office. Yeats and I drove across the island from Nanaimo to Tofino, stopping briefly at Cathedral Grove to see the trees. Cathedral Grove is part of MacMillan Provincial Park and is home to a stand of endangered, ancient Douglas firs and red cedars.

Some of the firs are eight hundred years old and the largest is more than nine metres in circumference. These trees are huge and tall and do create a cathedral-like atmosphere, but instead of immense stone pillars and high arched ceilings, the visitor is awed by these living objects reaching for the sky.

We walked around this surreal forest, following the trails with their ubiquitous signs reminding visitors to stay on the path. Yeats said, "It doesn't feel real. These trees, you can't see the tops of them. And there are no birds."

"No birds? Maybe there are birds and we just can't see them. Maybe if we stand still and listen, we'll be able to hear them."

"There are too many people. We'll never hear them." He was right. There were way too many other people—laughing and whining children, people shouting to one another when they found an even bigger tree "over here!" It was a cacophony.

We left shortly after and drove to the Pacific Ocean, one stunning view after another. Central Vancouver Island is mountainous and dotted with lakes, and the road follows the contours of all this natural beauty. We rounded a bend to see mountain peaks in the distance and then another bend to see a row of hills across a sparkling blue lake. I had to keep my eyes on the road, but luckily we were stuck behind some slowpoke camper vans, so I had time to look at the view. While Yeats scanned the sky for birds, I thought about the conversations I'd had with my girlfriends about where I belong.

My heart was torn in two.

We checked into Middle Beach Lodge in Pacific Rim National Park, on the very westernmost edge of Canada. The lodge was a ten-minute drive south from the town of Tofino and was perched on a cliff overlooking the ocean. From our window we looked out to a few small islands, which formed a breakwater for waves rolling in from an open sea. Beyond those islands, the next stop was Japan. I stood on our balcony above black rocks dropping in jags down to the shore, and felt the wind take my breath away. I had a feeling that this place could cure just about anything.

I took a look at the brochures I had picked up in the lobby.

I said, "Yeats, how about some birdwatching?"

I waved the brochure around. It had a black-and-white drawing of a tufted puffin on it.

He said, "Sure."

And that was the start of that.

GEORGE THE BIRDWATCHER PICKED us up at seven o'clock the next morning. He rolled down the window of his van and said, "Are you Lynn and son?" His cap was pushed back on his head and I guessed he was in his mid-sixties, his face well weathered from hours spent outside. I climbed into the front seat and Yeats into the back.

I said, "George, this is Yeats," and they shook hands between me. George did not offer me his hand.

He said, "Have you seen any birds here yet? Where do you bird-watch at home? What are your best birds?"

The whole time he was looking at Yeats in the rear-view mirror. He continued asking Yeats questions as we left the lodge and drove down the Pacific Rim Highway. Yeats gave mumbling, half-hearted answers but George was not deterred. He didn't look at me once.

In fact, for the whole morning, unless I asked him a direct question, George completely ignored me. Perhaps he sensed that Yeats was the "real" birder, or perhaps he was beyond thrilled to be given the opportunity to instruct a teenaged birdwatcher. I decided not to take it personally, not to see it as a slight on me or on women in general or on women nearing fifty in particular. I decided to blend into the background and enjoy the fantastic scenery.

We parked at a trailhead and George started talking about bird books. As we got out of the car, he told us (well, Yeats) that he preferred the Peterson guides because in those books you had many variations of the same bird on one page. "You see the adult male and female, adults in winter if they look different, juveniles, and so on. There are also pages in the Peterson where you get many warblers or sparrows together so you don't have to turn ten pages to find the one you're looking for when you're trying to identify a bird in the field."

He demonstrated this by opening his book.

He said to Yeats, "I always teach my students to use Peterson." He walked beside Yeats, stood in front of me, and gestured to the guidebook. I peeked over George's shoulder and saw a page filled with warblers.

George said, "See these? Colour bars. Look at the colour

bars on the wings, look for eye rings. Look for any distinguishing marks like that. Say them to yourself and then look at the book."

Yeats nodded and slipped me a glance. I smiled.

By now we were standing in front of a large expanse of deciduous trees. Yeats was looking around and George continued on, saying, "Once you get to know some birds, study their movements."

Yeats said, "There's one!" and lifted his binoculars. "I think it's a goldfinch."

George looked up as the bird flew deeper into the trees. He looked back down mumbling, "Good sighting." He said, "You'll get to know the birds by the way they move, how they hop or fly between branches, how they bob and weave."

"There's another," Yeats said.

George and Yeats looked through their binoculars at the trees, and I looked at them.

George said, "It's a Townsend's warbler. Nice sighting. See the colour pattern. Memorize that and then look at this page."

Before Yeats looked down at the book, he spied another bird. George sighed and they identified a Wilson's warbler.

"You're good," George said to Yeats. He didn't look at me. Maybe I wasn't there anymore.

The Townsend's warbler is a bird of the Pacific Northwest. It's a small black-and-yellow songbird with white wing bars. It winters in Mexico, where it eats, almost exclusively, the honeydew-producing scale insect—and it will vigorously defend its dining territory from other birds.

The Wilson's warbler is a small bird whose underparts are all yellow. The male, which we'd found here, has a black cap, and its nearly orange face is common in the western version. They are plentiful on Vancouver Island; we would go on to see many.

George gave a little lecture on recognizing birds by their voices, about memorizing their calls. Yeats listened to all these instructions but mostly he was watching for birds. George was too, but in a less pointed way. I had the feeling that George wanted to impart as much birding wisdom as he could to the younger generation as quickly as possible.

We walked down a seaside path and George talked about his younger days as a birder, how he and a couple of buddies used to skip school to look for birds. He was even more of a bird fanatic than Yeats. I looked at my son, who rolled his eyes. I could tell he wished George would be quiet and just show us some birds we'd never seen before.

We scrambled down to a beach strewn with boulders and giant logs. The sun was beginning to warm the air, but I kept my jacket zipped to my neck against the wind. Out beyond a small island, cormorants flew low to the water; two bald eagles turned in the clear sky high above us.

George set up his tripod, wedging it between the rocks. He turned the scope onto the small island and said, "Sometimes there are shorebirds over there. They're so perfectly camouflaged that you need a scope to see them."

Sure enough, he found a short-billed dowitcher, and we took turns looking at it through the scope as it pecked the ground, feeding.

The dowitcher is a medium-sized shorebird with a bill twice the length of its head. Its feathers are mottled browns and white, so it blends in with sand and rock and sky. To me its bill didn't look short at all, but the bird guide assured us that compared to the long-billed dowitcher's, it was short.

We watched the bird for a while and it seemed totally unaware of us. This was the first time we'd watched a bird through a scope. It was better than our binoculars because it was steadier and the magnification was greater. No matter how still you are, your binoculars will shake a bit, which can be annoying when you're trying to see the details of a new bird. (Are those black and white stripes on its wings, or is it a grey patch? Can't tell because my hands are shaking a teeny-weeny bit.) Also, the scope's greater magnification allowed us to see more detail at a farther distance — those gradations of colour along the wings, or that subtle shading around the eyes.

But the scope on its tripod was heavy and clumsy to carry. It was difficult to set up on uneven ground and, I imagined, grew heavier and heavier as the morning wore on. But I guess that was part of what we paid George for.

So far we had seen no other people on our tour, suiting us all just fine. As we moved along the beach to a little cove, George continued to tell us about his birding exploits, the tours he led in Peru and Ecuador during the winter, and all the places he'd been up and down the BC coast. George and I were stepping carefully over the sun-bleached logs, he with his heavy scope, binoculars around his neck, and pack on his back; I with my chronically unstable sacrum. (There were times when all I had to do was pick a sock up off the floor and my back would go out, and I didn't want to have to find a chiropractor on holiday.) Yeats was way ahead, striding over logs and rocks, long hair swinging. When we got to the cove, he was already standing there, a finger to his lips. That was for George, because I wasn't saying anything anyway.

"An oystercatcher," Yeats whispered, as loudly as he dared.

I looked to where he was pointing. The bird had lifted its head and was looking at us. George ceased his monologue and put the scope down without making a sound.

One minute I was ambling along enjoying the scenery and sea air, and the next I was stone-still, looking at a bird I'd only ever seen in a book. I'd seen it a thousand times in two dimensions in our Audubon guide to the birds of Western North America — another one of our favourites — young Yeats on my lap, the names of birds rolling off my tongue. I found that I'd memorized its shape, especially the shape and colour of its beak, which is bright red. This bird on the beach looked just like the one in the photo, but I probably wouldn't have been able to come up with the name "black oyster-catcher." I looked around. The beach was covered with rocks and driftwood, and the place smelled of piles of washed-up seaweed. The wind blew the scent of salt water to shore, and waves rhythmically swept the beach. Who wouldn't like to spend their time catching oysters and finding their fine-spun pearls, or just hanging out on a deserted beach where the next stop across the water was Japan?

George scanned the horizon with his binoculars and said, "There's lots more of them out there."

Oystercatchers were flying in a flock not too far out from shore, perhaps twenty individuals. Now we saw them standing on the rocky shore beyond the cove, pecking. Contrary to what their name suggests, their preferred foods are mussels and limpets.

I contemplated the bird nearest to us; I looked at my son, whose face was open and radiant. George was mercifully silent.

After the oystercatcher sighting George drove us back to our lodge where we packed up and checked out. Yeats and I drove back across the island to Nanaimo and stopped for lunch at a small campground. One bird we'd actively looked for in Tofino was the Steller's jay. We wanted to see it because it is so much like our blue jay from home, only bigger, and it is the only other jay in North America to sport a crest. The blue jay is gradually expanding its range west, and where the two birds overlap, they are interbreeding and creating hybrids. This hadn't happened on Vancouver Island, yet, so we were looking for the pure Steller, with its azure body and black head and crest.

The picnic tables at this rest stop were practically infested with Steller's jays. They scattered when we sat down but hopped on over as soon as we opened our lunch bags. They were gorgeous and saucy, just like our jays from Ontario, but we were a little shocked by how tame they were, and I was wary of their boldness. I shooed them away throughout our lunch and Yeats laughed at me. We'd finally found them and now I was trying to get rid of them.

THERE'S A BIG DIFFERENCE between watching birds and becoming a birdwatcher. The latter step involves binoculars, a birding destination, sometimes a guide, and at least one guidebook to birds, of which we'd always several, including the Audubons and the Royal Ontario Museum (ROM) and Sibley guides, though not the Petersons (sorry, George). It also involves keeping a list of the birds you've seen. Birders can be compulsive list-makers. Maybe most birders were always compulsive list-makers, even before they took up birding. Maybe birding is a good excuse for making lists. I don't know because I'm not compulsive that way, but Yeats is.

As a youngster, Yeats played complicated games with his toy cars and kept lists of the outcomes. He exasperated me with lists of dinosaur names; he made me play the dinosaur-alphabet game, where you had to name a dinosaur that started with each letter. He'd say Apatosaurus, I'd say Brachiosaurus, he'd say Corythosaurus, and so on. If I became stuck on M he refused to give me a clue, but made me sit there and think until I remembered Mamenchisaurus. He had deep faith that I'd get it eventually because of his own flawless memory, and I suppose it was that faith in me that kept me playing those games when I could have just walked away to make dinner. It was fun, in a strange kind of way.

As Yeats grew older he kept more and more lists. He

started keeping lists of all the music he listened to, all the songs and albums, all the artists and where they were from. When he was in Grade 7 my brother taught him how to make an Excel spreadsheet of all these music lists, complete with graphs and charts, and he updated them weekly, something he did for about a year.

When we arrived home from our trip to BC, Yeats started writing down the birds he saw on his walks around the city. He walked to and from home, across the Don Valley and through Riverdale Farm, stopping to look for birds. He kept the lists simple at first—just a notebook with the date on each page.

March 30: *house finch, dark-eyed junco, black-capped chickadee, American robin, blue jay.*

If it were me, I would have written *finch, junco, chickadee, robin*: the opening descriptor would have gone by the wayside in the name of convenience. But for Yeats, that wasn't accurate enough. There were too many kinds of chickadees and juncos to take such a cavalier attitude towards the lists. Eventually, he developed shortcuts: *A. robin*, for example, or *A. crow*.

After a while, too, he stopped writing down the five birds he saw every day no matter what: house sparrow, European starling, rock dove (pigeon to most of us), ring-billed gull, and American robin. They became the assumed birds.

Yeats reminded me of my mom's father, the geologist, who we called Bop. Bop made lists and charts and kept meticulous accounts of the world around him. He had an air of being grounded in time and space that Yeats carried, too. This quality is hard to define. I think it has something to do with being unhurried, and connected to the rhythms of the natural world.

Every once in a while Yeats would say, "Okay, Mom. Let's name all the birds we've ever seen." And he'd take out a piece of pristine white paper, his pencil, and his incredibly expectant look. I'd try really hard not to sigh and roll my eyes. Still, I was happy to encourage the birding after that successful trip to Tofino. I never once thought to myself, *Here is a good mother-son hobby*; it just naturally evolved into something that we did together. We developed our birding habits, our way of walking slowly through the forest, Yeats going first to set the pace. We didn't talk much — either in the car, where we listened to our favourite music, or in the field — and this companionable silence was part of what I loved about our trips.

BEN DID MANAGE TO take more holidays later that summer, August of 2008, when the stock market crashed. Economics has never been my strong point, but even I could tell this stock market problem was worse than the usual August downturn. Laurie's husband, Andy, gave us all a little lesson in bundled mortgages which I promptly forgot, and the daily paper was full of dire predictions for Canada and the world. People in the U.S. were losing their homes and giant brokerage houses were going under. It wouldn't be long before people on Bay

Street started losing their jobs, something that would slow our fledgling business right down.

Ben lay on a lounger on the cottage deck and read books, a book a day for the most part. He was famous for this. Once, when Lauren was three years old, she came around the corner of the deck to find her uncle reclining on the chaise with a book.

She spread her arms and said, "But why are you always lying there reading?"

He looked at her and replied, "But why are you always dressed in pink?" Some things just can't be questioned.

While Ben read his books, Yeats and I went to Wye Marsh for the first time. An old friend of my mother's had told us it was a great place to see birds. We ended up going there every summer, sometimes more than once.

Of all the places we went regularly to bird-watch, it was my favourite. At least once every trip, I'd stand on a little bridge over a stream and say, "I *love* it here." Yeats had the presence of mind not to say anything, and I'd follow as he stepped quietly off the bridge and back into the forest or out onto the marsh again.

The Wye Marsh Wildlife Centre inhabits 3,000 acres of land just outside Midland, Ontario. It's wetland, fen, and forest, operated as a non-profit society but in association with various environmental protection groups. They have an interpretive and education centre, boardwalks, an observation tower, canoe and kayak tours, bee-keeping, and a trumpeter swan restoration program.

That first visit, we drove down from the cottage early in the morning, and we were out on the boardwalk before the place officially opened for the day. We were alone in the marsh. Alone — except for thousands of creatures and countless cattails and a wisp of a wind blowing sweet, marshy smells over everything.

The marsh is a flat, grassy place. When the wind blew and we stopped to listen, we heard a soft whooshing as thousands of blades of grass rubbed gently against each other. And we smelled that incredible sweetness of fresh grass mixed with all the other things growing in the marsh — flowers, lily pads, the forest behind us.

We saw a lot of birds at the marsh. We were certain to see most of our old familiars: red-winged blackbird, great blue heron, black-capped chickadee, common yellowthroat. Seeing these birds over and over cannot be considered a waste of birdwatching time. Watching an American robin hopping down a path ahead of us was always a pleasure, and I never tired of seeing the yellowthroat, with its black eye mask, perching sideways on a reed and singing *witch-i-ty, witch-i-ty, witch-i-ty, witch*. Every bird at the marsh filled us with a little light. I wondered if I was just so simple that this was all it took. But then I thought, *I'm lucky that this is all it takes*, and knew that I was especially lucky that this was all it took for my teenaged son, too.

On one of the long, grassy pathways we saw a brown thrasher, a bird I remembered being described in one of our books as "a large, skulking bird of thickets and hedgerows."

We actually saw it in a hedgerow and it *was* skulking, making a positive identification difficult at first. We had to skulk along, too, bent over and sticking our necks out to see it from the path, trying not to scare it away. Brown thrashers are about the size of robins but have reddish-brown backs and white breasts heavily streaked with dark brown. They aggressively defend their nests and have been known to attack people and dogs forcefully enough to cause injury. It seems thrashers were well named, unlike those oystercatchers in BC.

We continued to the end of the pathway to a lookout shelter where we found a nest of young barn swallows. The parents were taking turns feeding the babies, flying out onto the marsh and then swooping back under the eaves of the shelter to fill the four open mouths. We sat for ages, mesmerized by these beautiful birds and their young.

I stood up and looked out from the shelter into the marsh, into acres of gently waving reeds and grasses. It was a scene that would never fail to fill me with tranquility, no matter how often I returned to it. Dragonflies, damselflies, butterflies: they all came to check me out. I especially liked the black-bodied damselfly, with its neon-green wings. I was looking through my binoculars, seeing nothing except the horizon, when a bird flew past.

"Yeats! A tern!" My favourite seabird. This one was a Caspian tern, the biggest tern in the world. I wasn't sure what it was doing there; maybe this one had decided to breed at the marsh. Maybe it had simply flown in for the day from

Georgian Bay. It was a beauty, though, and we watched it fly away over the grasses.

We walked back along the pathways and over the boardwalk that crosses the marsh, paying a visit to the little pond that houses the swans.

Wye Marsh started their trumpeter swan breeding program in 1989. In 1990, the first cygnet was born in captivity, and in 1993, this youngster and her mate were the first nesting wild trumpeter swans in Ontario in two hundred years. Since then, they have successfully bred year in and year out. While they are free to fly away and breed elsewhere, they often return to the marsh, where they have an enclosed area safe from predators such as foxes and dogs.

Trumpeter swans are the largest North American swan, with a wingspan that can exceed two metres. The adult has a black bill, which helps to distinguish it from the mute swan, whose bill is orange. The mute swan is an introduced species, from Europe, and is not mute at all. It is even rarer than the trumpeter swan, but is usually found in ponds and bays near people, so is more commonly seen by us.

We studied the four swans in the enclosed pond, trying to see their numbered tags. We had a vague plan to visit the Scarborough Bluffs or the Toronto Islands in winter to see if the swans there were the same ones at the marsh. It wasn't often you could say, "Hey, that's the exact same bird we saw last summer at the marsh!"

While Yeats memorized their numbers I looked for other birds. There were plenty of them, a bounty of red-winged blackbirds and song sparrows, American goldfinches and robins. I saw something land at the top of the fence and then quickly disappear into the bushes. Something grey and nearly as large as a robin. I described it to Yeats, who said, "grey catbird." My first grey catbird, so named for its mewling call.

We stood for a long time looking into the enclosed pond. We were on a covered dock, sheltered from wind and sun. It was a little like looking out at a diorama. We saw painted turtles on logs, frogs swimming between lily pads, catbirds flying from tree to tree, and these giant white swans swimming gracefully and nudging one another's necks.

All these common yellowthroats clinging sideways to the sky. All these swooping barn swallows. We sat on a bench along one of the walkways and waited some more. This was one of those scenes most of my friends couldn't envision: a teenaged boy sitting on a bench in a marsh with his mother, waiting for birds to come, no coercion involved.

We spoke very little. We raised our binoculars now and again, or drank from our water bottles. There were butterflies and frogs and crickets singing in the grass. We had nowhere to go and nothing to do. It was perfect.

FIVE

IN THE FALL OF 2008 we celebrated the bookstore's one-year anniversary by taking the staff out to dinner, all ten of us including our four children. Ben delivered a speech thanking everyone and we raised a toast to a fine first year. But it was a difficult time to be a small-business owner, to say nothing of trying to sell books. The markets had crashed, companies were shedding staff, the Canadian dollar was riding high. The media was full of stories of people living beyond their means, living on credit and deeply in debt. It was a fearful time and we weren't immune, as far as the business went. Everyone was looking for a deal, but we couldn't discount our books the way the big-box retailers could. (They couldn't, either, as it turned out. Actual books became a fraction, maybe as little as a quarter, of these giant shops' stock.) Nor could we compete with online retailers who offered books at a huge discount and delivered them to your house the next day, though we were happy to deliver, for free, in the downtown core.

As bleak as the outlook seemed for bookstores, with e-readers and other media joining the online shops in competing for people's time and money, Ben was optimistic.

"People have been predicting the demise of books since the advent of television, since before that," he said. "It hasn't happened yet and it won't happen this time, either."

He figured if we could get through this—an economic recession just a year after we opened in the heart of the financial district—we'd survive anything.

The first display I made in September was right in the entrance of the shop: a lovely selection of books about Zen and other forms of Buddhism. People were coming in for solace, looking for a sanctuary from the bad news out there, and I figured some of them needed to remember to breathe. We sold quite a few books from that display.

The biggest change for the family, however, was that Danielle went off to university. She was living in residence at King's College at the University of Western Ontario. This was in London, just down the 401, but it seemed like the other side of the country. Yeats missed her every single day. Danielle was Yeats's closest confidante, the person he could trust above all others with whatever he was thinking and dreaming, and now she'd committed herself to life in London for four years.

We missed her, too. She took the bus home for the occasional weekend, but everyone wanted a part of her—us, her mother, all her girlfriends—and we had to be content with a quick meal. She and Yeats spent dinner together comparing notes on Jarvis teachers. They talked about Yeats's new English teacher, Mr. Dewees. Yeats said Mr. Dewees was the first teacher who'd inspired him to *want* to work hard and to do well.

I asked him how this teacher differed from the others and he shrugged and said, "He just cares so much. He loves what he's doing. He makes it fun, but he expects a lot from us."

Danielle nodded and said, "He was like that for me, too. I took that Classics course not because I wanted to read those books, but because people told me he was an amazing teacher. He was. I never really expected to be so turned on by *The Odyssey*. I tried really hard in that course."

Yeats also talked about his art teacher, Mr. Simpson, who ran a creative, fun classroom. Yeats spent extra hours in the art room, learning how to stack the firing kiln and helping Mr. Simpson with displays and clean-up.

Yeats had never been into the party scene and that didn't change in high school. He didn't need to have something to do with friends on Friday and Saturday nights. The time spent in the art room, along with the poetry club, seemed to fill his social requirements, for the time being at least.

Showing my maternal concern I'd say, "Yeats, why don't you call one of your friends? Go to a movie or something. Have them over."

"Why would I do that? I get enough of them at school. Besides, all the movies my friends want to see are too violent or dumb."

"Maybe you could choose the movie. Maybe it would be fun to hang out with your friends. Go to a café in Kensington."

"I'm fine, Mom. You don't have to worry."

I should have known how he felt, loving solitude as I did, but in my teenaged years I was very social. I worried about my boy.

Titus and Rupert were living together in an apartment a bit east of us and since Rupert worked in the store, Ben and I saw him frequently. But Yeats was on a different schedule. Sometimes he came down to the store after school and read in the office or re-shelved the travel books, which always seemed to get out of order. He and Rupert would have a visit and sometimes they went off together to sell books at an event. Or maybe Yeats went off with Ben to sell books, or maybe he came home with me and we ate dinner and watched an old movie.

I had taken to renting Cary Grant movies, which we watched on the desktop computer on our third floor. And nearly every Friday night that fall, Ben joined us to watch something old and, hopefully, amusing. One night I rented *The Sound of Music*, which neither of them had ever seen. It seemed incredible to me that Ben could be fifty-nine years old and never have watched this classic movie. He spent the entire time trying hard not to mock it. A couple of times he said, "This is so cheesy...." then caught the expression on my face. He and Yeats exchanged about a thousand looks while I was happily reliving my childhood, when my family used to watch it every year on TV.

Despite these Friday movie nights, it was a struggle for us to spend time together as a family. We had dinner with all the boys, and Danielle if she was around, whenever we could, usually once or twice a month on a Sunday night. Ben would make a big pot of vegetable soup or cauliflower curry and we'd have leftovers the next day, although usually it would be just me eating the leftovers. Ben would be out selling books somewhere around town.

Grade 10 seemed to be suiting Yeats better. I felt that between Mr. Dewees and all the time Yeats spent in the art room, he was finding some kind of balance. His perennial dislike of the system was being tempered by a respect for individual teachers. But I knew that Yeats missed seeing Danielle and her friends every day at school. He consoled himself by walking home and listening to music in his bedroom.

WINTER IN TORONTO WAS a good time to see ducks. We chose a sunny Saturday in January and took the ferry over to Ward's Island, which is the easternmost part of Centre Island. This is the largest island in the chain that forms the Toronto Islands and helps to create the city's harbour. The boat carved a path through the loose ice and when I stood on the rear deck, I watched the ice close up behind us. The farther away we were from the city, the more it looked like we wouldn't be able to get back. The path was gone.

On the north side of the island we saw buffleheads and long-tailed ducks swimming in the harbour. We saw the ubiquitous black-capped chickadee on small trees near the ferry dock, but we didn't linger long. We crossed over, past a few island homes, towards the south side. There was no one about. Yeats had never been to this part of the Toronto Islands and was immediately charmed.

"People live here? In these little houses?" he said.

The houses were small and rustic-looking. They had wind-chimes and bird feeders and looked like my idea of West Coast hippie life, an idyll from my youth when I hung out in Kitsilano and went to that music festival every summer. But I worried the comparison was simplistic and silly, and didn't share it with Yeats.

He said, "Are there kids living here? Where do they go to school?"

"There's that island school, at the west side. The one your class went to when you were in Grade 5."

Children living on the island go to the Island Public/ Natural Science School, which was first established as a school in 1888. Children who live in the lakeside condos on the mainland join island dwellers every day for school, taking the ferry to and fro. And Yeats's class had joined them, too, for three days when he was ten. "Remember?" I asked him.

"Oh, yeah. It must be at the other end of the island. Maybe we'll get there today."

Before we knew it we were on the south side of the island, walking down to a sandy beach. The beach was covered with shattered ice shifting around in small waves. The sound was like a million ice shards tinkling in a huge glass bowl. I could have listened to it all day, but Yeats spotted something through his binoculars and wanted to see what it was.

A boardwalk runs along the south shore of Ward's Island, and from there we ended up seeing many species of duck. Most of them were out on the water, not close to shore. They were in large flocks, riding the freezing waves of Lake Ontario. We saw white-winged scoters, buffleheads, long-tailed ducks, female common mergansers, female red-breasted mergansers, common goldeneyes, redheads. When we moved in closer to shore we saw mallards and gadwalls.

It was cold in the wind but I was wearing a lot of clothes. I made a list of the layers in my head as I tried not to freeze: wool socks, boots, long underwear top and bottom, jeans, turtleneck, fleece, long down jacket referred to by my family as the "sleeping bag coat," hat, gloves, scarf. Yeats was wearing only sweatpants and his hoodie over a T-shirt, and running shoes on his feet. He put his arms through the sleeves of his down jacket but wouldn't zip it up until partway through the day when he finally started to feel the cold.

I said, "Why don't you do up your jacket? Where are your gloves? Do you want a hat?" I had an extra, inoffensive, hat in my backpack.

"I'm fine, Mom," he said, scowling a bit. The scowl was a warning not to push, which made me push just a little.

"But it's so cold. Aren't you freezing?"

"No. If I get cold I'll do up my jacket."

He turned his back on me and scanned the water for more ducks. He scanned the sky for geese. I took the hint and shut up. I made a conscious effort to lose my maternal irritation. Does a mother ever stop wanting her children to do things her way? Unlikely. But all we can do is hope that something has rubbed off over the years.

Mostly we walked without speaking, only piping up when one of us spotted something. It was our companionable silence, what I came to expect on these birding trips. Sometimes, in social situations, I found myself doing the same thing — watching rather than participating — and I wondered if it made some people uncomfortable. Probably it made them think I was a numbskull, with nothing to say. Oh, well.

We left the open lake and walked north along a road and past the Island School.

"See, this is it," I said. "You've even been here."

"I didn't know it was a regular school, too. I thought it was only a science school." He looked around. "It looks different at this time of year. We played a big game of Predator and Prey in a wood. I saw my first owl then. It was a great horned. I don't know where we were."

We looked for the spot but couldn't find it. We considered going down a road marked with a sign that said NO TRESPASSING, but decided not to. We walked a bit farther, east now, and saw a lot of wintering passerines: chickadees, cardinals, white-breasted nuthatches, house sparrows. It was sheltered there, so we sat on a bench and had a snack. A crow flew over, then another.

We walked again and eventually came to Centreville,

the summer amusement park on Centre Island. It was closed and deserted except for some animals in a farm across a small canal: a couple of donkeys, some sheep, and two large birds half-obscured by fencing. Yeats frowned and we walked down a pier that jutted into the canal.

"What are they?" I whispered. "Some kind of goose?"

"I don't know. They're a weird shape. It's hard to tell because of the fence."

"Maybe they're an accidental."

"Maybe." I heard both doubt and anticipation in this one word. Seeing an accidental is extremely exciting for a birder. You feel like climbing a rooftop and shouting it out, but first you have to be very sure.

A huge flock of mallards was swimming under a small bridge in the farm's canal. Their quacking was distracting me and I looked among them for other species.

Yeats started to laugh. He lowered his binoculars and said, "Look through your binoculars, Mom," but I didn't need to because one of the mystery birds had hopped onto the fence and I could see clearly that it was a peacock. I laughed too and caught Yeats's eye. His face was filled with glee at being caught out like that, the joke of it.

As we watched the peacock, a Cooper's hawk swooped in on the mallards, trying to grab one. The ducks made an enormous racket and then fell dead silent as they huddled together, squished like sardines under the bridge. The hawk tried again. We couldn't believe our luck to witness a hunt. We stood as still as statues, barely breathing. The hawk failed again on its third attempt, and we watched as it flew over the island and out over the inner harbour.

We walked the main road back to Ward's Island, the canal on our left. A bridge connected the road with more island houses, a different neighbourhood from the one we saw straight off the ferry.

"Do you want to cross over and walk down there?" I asked.

Yeats had a strange look on his face, one I couldn't read. I didn't think he was tired or in a hurry to get back to the city. This birdwatching trip had been relaxed, despite the cold, and I felt, once again, that these little expeditions close to home brought clarity to everyday life, in the way a holiday did. But a day spent birding on the Toronto Islands (or at Ashbridges Bay or High Park or Sunnybrook Park), cost next to nothing and took almost no preparation. We were refreshed precisely because we had stepped so easily outside our routine.

"Mom, this is the bridge!" His animation turned to frustration when it was obvious I didn't know what he was talking about.

"Which bridge?"

"The bridge. The one on the cover of *High Winds White Sky*, the Bruce Cockburn album. Let's see if we can find the exact angle of the photograph."

"When's the album from? The landscape may have changed. Different trees and so on."

"1971. Yeah, nearly forty years. But I think we can still find the spot it was taken from. It won't be that different."

Yeats was really focused, striding ahead with purpose. He loved that album.

"Is that your favourite album of all time?" I asked as we crossed the bridge and looked back at it, assessing angles.

"Who knows? Sometimes. It is when it's cold at the cottage and I make a fire and listen to it all wrapped up in my quilt, alone in the living room. Then it's my favourite."

I knew that scene. I'd walked past him into the kitchen to make coffee many times. He'd have pulled up a chair in front of the fireplace, ignoring me as I slipped past with freezing feet. Bruce would be singing of wind in the trees and birds gliding and of life beginning. It was a cottage sound for me, too.

We found the spot and felt immensely satisfied, as though we'd solved an age-old puzzle. Then we strolled back to the dock in silence. The day of birding had come to a meaningful close and we didn't need to talk about it.

On the ferry back to the city we saw a pair of mute swans fly past. In the distance some people were flying too, on their ice boats: catamarans on blades. People were playing hockey on the lake near the island shore and although I imagined I could hear the sounds of their sticks and skates on the ice, the ferry engine drowned them out. The ice opened for the ferry and closed behind it again. The cold wind chafed my face and I pulled my hat down further, covering my eyes with my sunglasses. I didn't want to sit in the cabin, so by the time we reached the mainland my brain was frozen along with my cheeks.

We left the ferry and I patted my pockets for my glasses and couldn't find them. A bit panicked, I said to Yeats, "I have to go back on the boat to find my sunglasses."

He laughed and said, "You're wearing them!"

I reached up, touched them, and laughed too, feeling very silly and suddenly much older. I knew he'd be teasing me about this one for years to come.

OUR THREE OLDEST KIDS, along with Danielle's friend Madison, went to Cuba for the 2009 Reading Week. At twenty-eight, it was Titus's first time at the ocean and he came back rejuvenated, expansive. I reminded him that when we took the rest of the family to Florida when they were youngsters, he didn't want to go. He didn't remember it that way; he thought we just didn't take him. But I remembered Titus, at sixteen or seventeen, declining our invitation. I didn't blame him at the time, thinking he'd be bored stiff playing in the sand and going to the Mote Marine Laboratory to pet stingrays. He was sure, though, that we had never asked him, so I apologized. I was mortified that he may have lived all this time with resentment or rejection or anger, and I was reminded of one of my father's favourite expressions: "Whoever said life was going to be fair?" *Parenting*, I thought to myself for the thousandth time, *is not for the faint of heart.*

Once the kids were back, we planned a birthday party for Ben. He was turning sixty in March, and we decided to celebrate at the house. I found an image of a psychedelic peace sign and used it as the background for a groovy e-mail invitation, which I sent out to sixty people. Ben always wore a peace sign pin on the lapel of his jacket—it was one of his trademarks. Almost everyone could come to the party, so I ordered an enormous round cake, which Yeats and I carried in its box to the basement.

During the party, Danielle helped me light the candles, the sixty of them arranged in the shape of a peace sign. When we turned out the lights, the table was lit by this fiery symbol of peace, and everyone fell silent as Ben tried to blow them out. He couldn't possibly do it in one go, so those of us who were gathered nearest to him helped.

Ben looked great at sixty. He said to me, "How do you feel being married to an old man?" He wasn't that much older than me—eleven years—but he joked that as long as I stuck with him, I'd always look good. I was planning on sticking with him anyway.

Still, all throughout that winter and into the spring I wasn't feeling so good. I was having trouble sleeping, sometimes lying awake for hours in the middle of the night, listening to the wind in the trees or to my thoughts going round and round. I blamed it on hormones. I was losing my mind along with my menses and all I wanted, half the time, was to be alone. Ben went to work and Yeats to school. I was blessedly alone in the house for a few hours (grocery shopping, laundry, and other household chores notwithstanding), so I sat on the couch with my book. The cat jumped onto my lap and demanded attention. He purred and looked at me with limpid eyes and I couldn't resist. I was a sucker for someone to look after, but I also felt myself getting sick of it.

One night I had a dream that I was embarking on a trip and I needed to strap everything I was taking onto my body. I was tremendously encumbered; I was hunched over with the weight of the stuff. I looked in a mirror and saw that I had two huge stuffed animals slung over my shoulders. I pulled them off and felt so much lighter. Of course, the meaning was clear: I was carrying around something from an earlier part of my life that I no longer needed; once I saw what it was and let it go, I'd feel better. Perhaps the meaning also had to do with supporting other people in my life, the fact that I carried around an outsized idea of responsibility towards Ben and Yeats, and even my step-children, whom I worried about without expressing it. Perhaps it was time to re-examine the expectations I had for myself in all these relationships and learn to let go a bit.

The really funny part was this: the next morning, Yeats and I left the house together and found a giant teddy bear sitting on a neighbour's garbage can. The bear looked brand new, and we heard the garbage truck on the next street over.

Yeats said, "We can't leave it here for landfill. Look at it—it's so cute. Let's take it home and give it to Noah." Noah is my youngest nephew.

I thought about my dream and said, "Do you think he really needs it?"

Yeats looked at me and said, "We can put it straight into the trunk of the car. It doesn't need to come into the house."

He knew me well. I sighed and popped open the trunk and in went the enormous bear that someone had probably won at the midway at the CNE.

I marvelled at the energy that moved us all. I marvelled at a universe that showed me an excess of stuffed animals in a dream and then presented me with a giant one free for the taking three hours later. I knew I should have resisted that bear, but the whole thing amused me so much that I couldn't.

Later that week I decided I needed to get rid of some stuff. We all had so much stuff. I sorted through closets and drawers and made a triage. It felt so good. I decided I wanted to dispose of some of my journals, take them to the cottage and have some kind of ritual burning. These were my morning pages, years of them, and I was tired of wondering why I kept them. Did I want someone to read them when I was gone? By then there could be a whole house full of them. Did I want to burden someone with that task? I decided I would take a bag of thirty or so journals to the cottage and burn them, in twos and threes, over the course of several weekends. Yeats was dismayed at first, but he couldn't dissuade me. They were mine, after all.

SIX

WE WERE IN MUSKOKA the first weekend of October, 2009.
Yeats was in Grade 11. Fall colours were coming on, crisp air.
My brother's family and my mom were also up north, but they
were over at the new cottage. Ben, Yeats, and I breakfasted
together around the big round wooden table, watching red
squirrels chase each other, listening to blue jays calling.

Yeats was upset and restless because David Dewees, his
Grade 10 English teacher and Danielle's Grade 12 Classics
teacher, had been accused, in the press at least, of inappropri-
ately touching an eleven-year-old boy at a summer camp. The
story had broken when the police came to the school that past
Thursday. Mr. Dewees had been suspended from the Toronto
District School Board until further notice and was staying
at his parents' house. He was Yeats's favourite teacher and

beloved at Jarvis because of his infectious enthusiasm for the subjects he taught, for books, and for people. He was young and could relate to the kids. He had suggested that Yeats read *A Prayer for Owen Meany*, which he had, over the summer. It blew his mind. In September Yeats went in to see Mr. Dewees to thank him and to ask for more book recommendations. Mr. Dewees told him to come back and he'd give him a list of more great novels to read. Then this happened.

Yeats said, "He can't be guilty of this. None of us believe it. It just isn't true. He isn't like that at all."

Ben said, "Maybe it's been wrongly reported. Maybe the charges are wrong. Maybe it isn't abuse, but enticement or something like that."

I nodded, but Yeats gave him a disgusted look.

"Even that couldn't be true. What does that even mean? I'm sure he's innocent and the newspapers just want to sell more copies so they say anything they want." Yeats paced in the kitchen for a while then came to sit back down. He said, "We're going to make a video for him. A whole bunch of us. We're going to let him know we think he's innocent and how much we're on his side. We want him to know that."

"When will you do this?" I asked.

"Monday at school. First thing. Then we'll send it to him. He won't be at school."

The phone rang and I picked it up. It was Danielle calling from university, four weeks into her second year. The sound of her voice when she said, "Hi Lynn, how are you?" made me think she'd called because things weren't going well for her. That she needed to talk about school. But what she had to tell me took my breath away. I sat down on the living room couch and put my head on the coffee table. I was bent right over, the phone to my ear, listening to my lovely stepdaughter tell me how Mr. Dewees killed himself.

She said, "He jumped in front of a train, at High Park station. He snuck out of his parents' house and walked over there." Her voice was tight and controlled and full of sadness. "It was yesterday. We can't believe it. He is...was...such a great guy. We all loved him." A crack in her voice.

"What about you? Are you okay? Are you going to come home?" I said.

"I'm okay. I'm here with Madison. We'll both come home for the funeral. Tell Yeats that." Madison had been Danielle's closest friend since Grade 2 and they were rooming together at university. They supported one another through all of life's trials and I was glad to hear they were together and would be home to support Yeats, too.

But now I had to pass on this piece of dreadful information to Ben and Yeats. They could tell, of course, that something awful had happened and both looked at me expectantly when I said goodbye to Danielle.

"What?" Yeats said.

I closed my eyes and took a breath.

"That was Danielle. Mr. Dewees killed himself. Yesterday. He jumped in front of a subway." We later learned that he'd lain down on the track and waited for a train to run him over. Such anguished deliberation.

Ben said, "Oh God."

Yeats stared at me. I put my head on my arms on the table and cried. Not sobs, just quiet tears in a steady stream. I looked up as Yeats pushed back his chair and left the table.

"Yeats?"

He waved his hand at me as he left the room, pushed open the screen door, and walked out into the forest.

THE REST OF THE weekend passed in a dream. I broke the news to my family and then tried to commiserate with Yeats, but he didn't want to talk. He spent nearly every waking hour in the forest.

We drove back home to Toronto, and Yeats and his friends, and Danielle and hers, went to the funeral. They said the church was packed, standing-room only, and everyone was crying.

David Dewees had taught the enriched English class for kids who wanted an extra challenge. His particular strength was in making the class exciting, in ramping up the kids' love of reading and writing. Yeats said his classes were never boring — high praise from a teenaged boy who hated school. For one of their projects, Mr. Dewees had them each read a book of their choice, an adult novel. Yeats read *Life of Pi* by Yann Martel. Instead of writing an essay on their book, the class pushed all the desks aside, brought in juice and snacks, and they had a "cocktail party." The idea was to spend the period going around and chatting about the books they'd read. Mr.

Dewees circulated among them, listening and asking questions and generally being enthusiastic. His enthusiasm was contagious, a gift to his students.

Our kids were steaming mad at the press, and questions flew around the dinner table and all over their social media about the lack of justice in the reporting of Mr. Dewees's case. There were countries in the world where the press was allowed to report a name and an arrest, but no details and certainly no speculation before a trial. Why was our media permitted to prematurely blacken someone's reputation like this? The consensus among Mr. Dewees's friends was that, guilty or innocent, he wouldn't have survived the stigma, that he was anguished by the publicity and the thought that he might never be allowed to teach again.

We talked about that, about fragility and culpability. We talked about what it meant to be bullied by the press and bullied in the on-line community. This was a horrible, visceral lesson for all of us. I called the school and talked to David Reed, Yeats's mentor, who was an English teacher, like Mr. Dewees, and a close friend of his.

David said he'd keep an eye on Yeats. He said he saw Yeats every week at Art Beat and I knew this would be a comfort for Yeats. Mr. Reed had a calm and unhurried manner, and the kids knew he cared for them. Yeats said Mr. Reed seemed to understand what it was like to be at high school; he was filled with empathy. David told me that the English department was in shock and I could see that my boy was in shock too. He was always complaining of being tired and I explained how exhausting grief was and that even when he was over the worst of it, every once in a while it would come crashing back. He cried and I comforted him. He didn't do his homework and I didn't press. He said they had an English test and everyone failed, the entire class. The teacher threw the tests out.

In November we went in for the parent-teacher interviews and nearly every teacher talked about Mr. Dewees and the impact his death had had on the school community and on Yeats in particular. I nodded and cried quietly.

The science teacher, on the other hand, was all business. She showed Ben and me a graph of Yeats's marks, and I pointed to a zero and asked what happened there. She said there was an assignment that he didn't hand in. I looked at the date and saw that it was due in mid-October. I explained to her how devastated Yeats was by Mr. Dewees's death and she looked crushed. She made a note in her book to take that zero off his record.

YEATS WENT BIRDWATCHING ON his own. This was the start of his letting go of me, and as sad as I was to see him miserable and alone, I didn't push. He went over to the Brickworks or down to Ashbridges Bay. The Brickworks is a park in the Don Valley that had been made from Toronto's pre-eminent brickyard. It has ponds and grassy hillsides as well as heritage buildings and a gateway to the Beltline, an urban forested trail. Ashbridges Bay Park is on the Toronto waterfront and is comprised of beaches, trails, groves of trees. Yeats walked home from school and stopped in Riverdale Farm to look for birds. He took solace in being alone in nature, even in the middle of the city. I understood that he needed to make sense of his loss as well as all the attendant anger. For him, bird-watching was the place to do that.

For birdwatching is a place, not just an activity. It's a place I knew I could go to in my mind when day-to-day life seemed overwhelming. I could remember seeing ducks bob-bing on the frozen waters of the outer harbour, for example, and feeling my blood pressure drop. I saw that place in my boy as I watched him go out to heal his spirit. He shoved his binoculars into his pocket and slipped into that place where he looked for birds, into that corner of his being. He was so unhappy and vulnerable, trying to understand a part of life that we, as parents, would rather shelter our children from as long as possible. But I knew he'd be okay because along with the vulnerability, Yeats possessed an emotional intel-ligence that would see him through. He threw himself into birdwatching, for example, rather than into risky behaviour that might end badly. This comforted me especially because I was busy with the store. It was October, which meant the ten-day international literary festival and then November, which was filled with book launches and events outside the store, and then the build-up to Christmas when I needed to work more shifts. I couldn't be there, physically, for Yeats the way I'd been when he was small, even if he wanted me to be.

But then, one day, he asked me if we could go to Amherst

Island to look for owls during the Christmas break and I was delighted. I knew he needed me for my car but that was okay. I needed to go birdwatching, too. I'd been craving it. But my birdwatching place included Yeats.

AMHERST ISLAND IS LOCATED at the east end of Lake Ontario, very close to Kingston. At seventy square kilometres, it's one of the latgest islands in all of the Great Lakes, and lies directly in the path of one of the world's biggest bird migration routes. The island is largely a farming community, but in recent years it has attracted mainlanders wanting either a second home on the island or a permanent residency. We'd heard about it from a bookstore customer who lived there. Browsing in the store one day, he mentioned something to Ben about seeing owls in his backyard in winter and about all the different hawks he saw when he went for a walk. I looked up Amherst and saw there was an area on the island called Owl Woods. This sounded promising.

Yeats tucked that information away and pulled it out in late October.

"When can we go?" he asked, during the IFOA when I was too tired to think.

I said, "Christmas. We'll go at Christmas."

"Will Ben come too?"

"Probably not."

All four of Ben's children called him Ben, not Dad. Every once in a while one of the three older ones would call him

Dad and to my ears it sounded endearing, as though they were feeling particularly close to him in that moment. When I asked Ben why they didn't call him Dad, he shrugged and said, "Titus just always called me Ben, maybe because that's what his mom called me. Then the rest of the kids did, too." When I pressed, asking if he never wanted to be called Dad, he shrugged and said, "Not really. I am Ben."

Ben liked to bird-watch but not in winter. He didn't have boots or a winter jacket. He refused to wear gloves, a hat, or a scarf. He was famous in our neighbourhood for wearing his suit jacket and jeans, no matter the howl of the wind or the depth of the snow. So I couldn't count on him for winter walking. Plus, he was too busy at the store. Even in the spring, when we were going somewhere close to home like Sunnybrook Park or the Leslie Street Spit, he seldom came with us. I understood the busy schedule, but I thought he might benefit from an occasional walk in the woods. Sometimes it made me sad that Ben didn't come along, but to be honest, Yeats and I enjoyed being alone together on these outings.

I had been praying for clear weather and we got it. We drove the three hours to Millhaven, just west of Kingston, and then took the fifteen-minute ferry ride across to Amherst. I loved putting my car on a ferry, no matter how short the ride, and leaving the mainland behind. I loved being on an island.

We could see Wolfe Island with its armies of wind turbines on the crossing, as well as all kinds of wintering ducks: common goldeneyes, red-breasted mergansers, buffleheads, mallards, lots of Canada geese. We'd come to see the owls, but tundra swans were supposed to be hanging around in the freezing lake, just off the east coast of the island. We hoped to see them, too.

Amherst Island was on the cusp of acquiring wind farms like those on Wolfe Island just across the water. We saw signs on people's lawns proclaiming their stance against the turbines. Their concerns, we knew, centred around health (the noise, the vibration), and the disturbance of nature (the birds, the fragile limestone bedrock). Our friends had told us that the dispute was in danger of fracturing the community into two camps. It wasn't exactly long-time farmers versus recent or seasonal residents, but close to it. Some of the turbines were to be placed next to Owl Woods, where snowy owls winter and several owl species spend summers. Our friends said they could talk to us all day about the dispute and we wouldn't believe half of what they had to say. For example, farmers on Amherst who wanted turbines on their land had to sign an agreement, not only not to talk to anyone about their own contracts but also not to talk to anyone else who already had turbines. (In 2013, the power company has requested permission from the province to disregard any endangered species on the island when finalizing its proposals.) It all sounded crazy to me.

Amherst was a very sleepy place in January. The hamlet of Stella was deserted. The few cars and pickup trucks that were on the ferry with us dispersed and disappeared. There were no shops or cafés. Even the store with the post office sign seemed to be closed. The school, too, was closed since it was still Christmas break, making the place feel even more like a ghost town.

As we drove across the island, though, we began seeing people here and there. We saw farmers around their barns and the occasional person out for a walk. We saw people walking their dogs and others filling their bird feeders. Everyone waved at us, something we were not used to in the big city. I waved back, gleefully.

Amherst is mostly rolling fields with a few small areas of brush and forest. There are homes and cottages along the shoreline and the one little town of Stella. About four hundred people live year-round on the island and another four hundred or so join them in summer.

For most of the day, ours was the only car in sight. It was lovely. It meant we could drive as slowly as we wanted, keeping a lookout for birds or a good place to stop. It meant I could pull over in an instant and park at the side of the road. We left the car unlocked as we ventured into fields and copses of trees. Despite being the middle of winter, there was only a light layer of snow on the ground and none on the roads.

We turned onto the main road out of Stella. To the left were houses overlooking the lake and to the right were fields bordered by an occasional thicket. Just past the last house Yeats spotted movement in a clump of trees, so we stopped and got out. We saw a northern cardinal and a blue jay along with a whole flock of dark-eyed juncos. We saw these birds in our backyard every day, but it was still worth the stop.

The whole time we'd been investigating these birds we'd

been hearing the persistent honking of a lone goose on the lake side of the road. We crossed over to take a look.

The lake was frozen from the shoreline to about 250 metres out. A flock of Canada geese was swimming around, but one poor goose was frozen in the ice. It was this bird that was making all the racket, and we saw instantly that it wasn't just because it was stuck and uncomfortable. A red fox was slowly advancing on it. The goose struggled and honked, pulled and pulled, trying to get free. Its compatriots kept swimming around. I was thinking they could have flown at the fox, driving it off. I didn't know why they wouldn't do that. Maybe this stuck individual was a particularly annoying goose. Maybe they were waiting for the fox to get closer.

The fox sat down and licked a paw. The goose squawked. The fox looked around, stood up, sat back down again. It advanced a bit and sat down again. Maybe it was waiting for the goose to get really tired before it went in for the kill. We decided we didn't want to see the kill and went back to the warm car.

We drove to the end of the island and turned south, the only way the road went. Someone had planted a huge purple martin house in their garden near the road. We fantasized about seeing purple martins swooping in and tucking themselves into this house. It was the wrong time of year, though. The martins were somewhere down in South America.

We continued down the road until we noticed a little break in a fence and a footpath snaking along the shore.

I parked the car again and we took the footpath, hoping it would lead us to the swans.

We were walking in shallow snow and some slush, which didn't bother me in my winter boots. It didn't bother Yeats in his running shoes, either, but it bothered me that Yeats's feet were probably getting wet. Like father, like son. This was an endless source of irritation between us. I cared about his feet way more than he did. If people could see Yeats's father's feet, they would understand. I wouldn't wish Ben's feet on anyone and neither would he — corns, bunions, in-grown toenails, horrible old sports bruises on his ankles that have never healed. They are a mess. So I feared that Yeats's cavalier attitude towards his wet, cold feet in winter was the first step towards feet like Ben's, even with the assurance of friends that this was normal teenaged behaviour. To be fair, Yeats did wear his orthotics religiously. He'd inherited his father's flat feet (and his hard head).

Waves were crashing on our right and the freezing wind was blowing into our faces, but we were happy to be outside looking for giant white birds. The field was to our left, looking empty and frozen, but Yeats spied something moving and we stopped to look. It was a snow bunting. Then it was a whole flock of snow buntings, rising from the snow-dusted field where they'd sat camouflaged. We watched as a couple dozen birds flew and swooped around the field together, their little white wings flashing in the sunlight. It was a magnificent sight and all the better for being unexpected. Over the years this would become an iconic birding moment for us, one we would pull out whenever we were talking about our best sightings or the times that most delighted us.

Snow buntings resemble sparrows in size and shape, and in fact they were once classified as sparrows, but are no longer. Now they are classified with longspurs, another family of perching bird. Buntings in winter are white and sandy-coloured. As a flying flock, they appear all white, but they aren't. The males will leave the relative warmth of these fields in April, about six weeks ahead of the females, and will begin building nests somewhere in the Arctic at temperatures as low as −30°C.

Our next stop was inland: Owl Woods. There were no signs, but the map I'd downloaded indicated that the woods were off the first road that bisected the island, heading west. We bumped along that road until we arrived at a bend where two other cars were parked. On one side of the bend was a house and on the other was a trailhead with a signpost of rules. A bit farther on was a board with descriptions of flora and fauna, but nowhere was there a map of how to get to Owl Woods.

We followed the footpath and trusted it would take us there eventually. It led to a scrubby forest full of black-capped chickadees looking for handouts (which we happily supplied in the form of oatcake crumbs), as well as some of our other winter woodland friends — downy woodpeckers, white-breasted nuthatches, a blue jay, juncos.

We came to a clearing and across it was an evergreen forest with little bits of colour here and there — other birders in their down jackets and toques. This was our destination.

We hiked until we found ourselves in a small clearing where the snow was trampled down. I saw a pine tree with wide, spreading limbs and little clusters of needles. In every cluster sat a perfect ball of snow about the size of a toddler's fist. I couldn't stop looking at this joyful sight, this tree flooded with sunlight, decorated by nature.

We preferred being still in the woods. We looked up, moved slowly and quietly, searching for owls. We hoped that those other people didn't come any closer with their loud whispers and crunching feet.

Three owls swooped soundlessly out of the woods. One flew on while the other two doubled back and landed somewhere in the pines, hidden and silent. We stood still again, breath held, sun pouring into the clearing. We waited and I felt my limbs grow loose; I felt my breath relax and my feet planted.

After a couple of minutes I beckoned to Yeats to stay put in the clearing. He nodded and I moved into the trees, quiet as a mouse, only little crunchings of snow and the slidy sound of my nylon jacket brushing a branch. Within fifteen seconds I saw them, high in a tree: two owls. I turned my head back towards the clearing and called, "Yeats, come." He moved even more quietly than I had; he could be a tracker. He stood beside me and I signalled up with my eyes.

There sat two long-eared owls, one facing us and the other sitting right beside the first but facing the opposite direction. We watched through binoculars as, very slowly, this second owl turned its head all the way around to face us too. Two owls staring at us staring at them. We watched each other for fifteen seconds before they flew away. We lowered our binoculars and looked at one another. My wonder was reflected in my son's face and we both smiled.

The long-eared is a medium-sized owl, about the size of a crow. It's widespread throughout most of North America at least some of the year, but not commonly seen. It hunts at night—studies have shown that it has supreme hearing and can catch mice in the pitch dark—and stays hidden in the woods during the day. We were lucky to have seen these two. Later that day we saw a snowy owl perched on top of a hydro pole just outside Stella. Yeats saw it as I was driving.

"Stop!" he shouted. "A snowy!"

We climbed out of the car, leaving the doors open, and stood gawping at the bird. We had no need of binoculars, we were so close. It stared at us for twenty seconds then swooped off.

"Listen," Yeats whispered behind me. The snowy was absolutely soundless; large white wings tipped with grey, flapping as though in a silent movie.

The snowy owl is unmistakable, being the only white owl around. It nests in the Arctic and, though it winters in most of the Canadian provinces and the northern United States, seeing a snowy is not easy. It, too, usually hunts at night, and tends to live in secluded areas. Its preferred food is lemmings, and in years when the lemming population is low, it will migrate as far south as Alabama and Georgia. Seeing a snowy was a heady experience. It filled me with a kind of awe and I wanted it to happen again.

Another favourite moment on Amherst was seeing the bald eagle. This time we only saw the bird in flight, but what a sight it was. We watched until we couldn't see it any more as it flew out over the fields. Yeats made an audible sigh behind me as he lowered his binoculars. This was a sigh of deep satisfaction. He nodded at me and we got back in the car.

As we drove back to the city, I thought of how priceless moments like these were. They became etched into our memories and didn't cost us anything except transportation and time. To be standing together in a frosty field, looking up into the sky, marvelling at birds and revelling in the natural world around us, was a simple miracle. And I wondered why we were so rarely able to appreciate it.

SEVEN

YEATS DID A LOT of birding in a short period of time and I accompanied him when I could. We'd get up on a Saturday morning and Yeats would say, "Can we go to the Brickworks today?" An hour later we were zooming down the Bayview extension and minutes after that, we were slowly walking the pathways over the ponds. We were looking for hawks, hoping for goldfinches.

Or Yeats would have a half-day of school, and we'd hop in the car after lunch and drive to Humber Bay Park or High Park or Sunnybrook Park or Ashbridges Bay. We were lucky to have so many places to go in Toronto. As winter turned to spring, we saw more species — a northern mockingbird at Humber, a spotted sandpiper at Ashbridges.

Whenever he returned from one of his solitary expeditions,

Yeats would list all the birds he'd seen. He listed them in his book and also out loud for me. He brought out his bird guides to show me which birds he'd seen. He talked about their migration routes and where they'd be nesting in the spring and when they'd be leaving to migrate south. He talked on and on and at some point, I tuned out. Well, I didn't tune out completely, but I didn't pay as much attention as I thought I should.

The truth was, while I loved going out to see birds, to be alone with him like that, I was not too fanatical about all the details. He could tell me a hundred times where the spotted sandpiper nests in Ontario and I wouldn't remember the next day. Such a big part of why I loved birdwatching was being in the moment, really *being* in the forest or on the sand spit or sitting overlooking a marsh. The actual bird details I left to the boy. That was just the truth of it.

Later that winter, our datebook was starting to fill with spring publishing events. I had a long list of things to do before mid-March, so I couldn't go birding as often as I would have liked. Yeats seemed to prefer going on his own, anyway, especially in the rain. And we had a trip coming up that required planning. There were a million things I needed to pick up — duffle bags from a friend, extra memory and batteries for the camera — and I had to speak to our friend Holly, who would be staying in the house to look after the cat. We were going to a place that is every birder's dream: the Galapagos Islands.

A few weeks into autumn, Laurie had called from Greenwich and said, "What are you guys doing for March break?

Because we're going to the Galapagos, to sail around for a week, and we have three extra spots on the boat. Wanna come?"

It was a Sunday morning and we were having breakfast. I put my hand over the receiver and said to Ben, "It's Laurie. They're inviting us to go with them to the Galapagos. Let's say yes."

Ben looked stunned. It isn't every day you get an offer like this. He was caught off guard and said, "Jeepers. Okay. That would be amazing. How can we turn that down?"

I eyed him carefully and said to my sister, "Yes. We'd love to join you. Thanks a lot." It was decided: we were going on a big trip—Ben included.

IN THE AIRPLANE ON the way to Ecuador, Yeats asked me which bird I most wanted to see.

I replied, "Albatross." Yeats glared at me because he knew that I knew we wouldn't be seeing an albatross. It was the wrong season for albatrosses in the Galapagos Islands, something he'd been telling me for the past few months. We'd had a long time to contemplate this voyage.

Ben said he wanted to see the booby, entirely tongue-in-cheek because he knew it was what we expected him to say. Parents are so irritating.

"Okay, then," I said, "I most want to see something I don't even know about yet. Otherwise," I continued, catching Yeats's stony look, "I want to see the magnificent frigate-bird with its red throat."

This was an acceptable answer and, as it turned out, we would see those frigates, lots of them, more than we could ever imagine and up so close we would swear they must be tame.

We were accidental tourists to the Galapagos. This was not a trip we had ever dreamed we'd take. It was my brother-in-law Andy's trip, planned by him and for his family. But they had those three extra spots on the boat and we were filling them.

The group convened in Guayaquil, Ecuador's largest city, which was located on the coast: very hot, very muggy. For Ben and Yeats, who had never been to a developing country, it was magnificently exciting. The traffic alone, with five lanes accommodating eight lanes of cars, food and drink vendors wending through the vehicles, no visible means of control anywhere, not to mention the apparently life-threatening taxis we took, yielded story after story over many a dinner to come. The mix of colonial architecture with modern; the tired, run-down feeling of most of the city juxtaposed with the incredible energy of the place; the wonderful Malecón — the boardwalk — along the waterfront; the marketplace... our trip was off to a memorable start.

We checked out Iguana Park, across from the main cathedral in the centre of town. Land iguanas languished and lolled and then crawled all over one another at feeding time, each trying to out-eat the other. They looked prehistoric, somehow unreal, and I was reminded of a stuffed iguana Mom and Dad had brought home from a trip to Mexico when I was a kid. My brother kept it in his room for years until it started to rot and its claws broke off.

We saw birds we couldn't identify — beautiful little blue ones that Yeats thought must be some kind of tanager — and small doves like our mourning dove but with different colouring. We saw grackles and a kind of tropical kingbird and hummingbirds. There were too many kinds of hummingbirds in Ecuador for us to even begin to identify them. In fact, there were too many kinds of birds in Ecuador, period, for us to identify them. I'd looked for a bird book before the trip. The only one available came in two volumes, each one over $100 and weighing ten pounds. So we'd bought a general guidebook for the Galapagos instead.

From the Malecón we saw three kinds of heron down at the river's edge: black-crowned night heron, yellow-crowned night heron, and striated heron. The first two we remembered from our faithful Audubon field guide at home, and the third was in our Galapagos book. At first glance I couldn't see any birds and wondered what Yeats and Ben were talking about. Then my eyes adjusted and I spotted them. The night herons are smaller, more compact, than the familiar great blue. They blended in with the riverbank, but as soon as I saw one, I started to see them all over the place. The birds were poking about in the mud and plant debris while the river rushed by on its way to and from the sea. I could have stood and watched that river all day, except that the weather was far too hot. We bought bottled water and found some shade in a small treed garden where hummingbirds were feeding off a flowered vine covering a rock wall.

All told, sixteen people were on the trip: Laurie, Andy, and their children, Thomas and Lauren; Andy's oldest brother, Stephen, and his wife Jane; Andy's sister Barbara, her husband Tom, and their seven-year-old daughter Fiona; Andy's younger brother David and his wife Meredith; and Andy's parents, Ron and Barb. And us. Steve and Jane, and David and Meredith each had three children, but they were at home.

We'd known all these Chisholms for years and felt relaxed and welcomed amongst them. The night before the departure to the islands, we went out for a celebratory dinner. All sixteen of us sat at a long, narrow table and made a toast: to Andy, to family, to tropical adventures. Yeats and his cousin Thomas were ecstatic to be travelling together, and I laughed watching them goon around at the table. Lauren and Fiona acted likewise, faces shining. The adults were more circumspect in their emotional displays, but clearly we were a happy bunch.

We flew from sunny Guayaquil to the Galapagos Islands, where it was pouring rain. We met our guide, Jorge, who told us as soon as we were seated on the bus that our boat, the *Alta*, wasn't ready. He'd take us to a different, more luxurious boat, which would ferry us to the *Alta* after dinner. So far we'd nearly missed our connection to Guayaquil from Bogota due to overbooking; two of our bags (one of ours and one of Jane's) were lost and returned to us only hours before the flight to the Galapagos; and now this new glitch. Some of us looked at Andy, who just smiled and shook his head.

We liked Jorge, though. The delay wasn't his fault. He knew his flora and fauna, and he was a professional photographer with an eye for what was interesting. We ended up learning a lot from him.

The *Alta* was a 46-metre ship with three masts. Most of the time we were under engine power, but from time to time they raised the sails and we flew across the water, dolphins leaping at the bow. That was a good memory.

The sixteen of us slept two per cabin, and there were nine crew, including Jorge. The young girls bunked in together, across the narrow hall from Yeats and Thomas. Both sets of children managed to personalize their cabins within hours of being on board: stuffed animals for the girls and stuff everywhere for the boys. We all settled in pretty quickly and had a good first night on the ship.

Over the course of the week we would cruise from island to island, stopping from time to time to hike or snorkel or play on a beach. We were there in March, so the weather was variable: a little rain every day and a lot sometimes, but only in the afternoons. The currents brought warm water at that time of year, so the swimming was lovely.

The most exciting birds for me were the ones that followed the boat and those that landed high up in the rigging for a ride. These were the storm petrels, the frigate birds, the tropic birds. They had huge wingspans and curved beaks and lived for months at sea. In my romantic imagination they were impossibly free. I sat on the upper deck in the sunshine watching them fly around the masts.

We saw the red-billed tropic bird once and the magnificent and great frigate birds every day. These birds accompanied us for hours at a time, sometimes flying with the boat and sometimes perched in the rigging. Both species are about 102 centimetres long, which is about the length of a large Canada goose. The tropic bird is white with a red bill and has long white streamers flying off its tail, making it look twice as long as it is. The frigate bird is black; the males have their distinguishing red throats while the females have white breasts. Jorge told us that some of the frigate birds were Greats, because they had a pale wing bar. All frigate birds, he said, spent almost their entire lives at sea, but they rarely, if ever, landed on the water.

Yeats didn't spend a lot of time on deck. Instead, he passed hour after hour in his cabin with Thomas, where they played cards and a game involving tossing a tissue box up into the porthole. They joined us on all the expeditions and went snorkelling, but when the boat was moving from island to island, sometimes for long stretches at a time, they were downstairs.

I said, "What about joining us on deck? It's beautiful up here. The breeze is amazing. There are dolphins and frigate birds. We've come a long way for this." What I didn't say was: *we haven't come all this way for you to spend so much time in a dark cave.*

He said, "It's too hot. You know I don't like the heat. It's

March! It's not supposed to be hot in March! Besides, I thought you wanted me to spend more time with my cousin."

"You guys are down there with the air conditioning on?"

"Yes."

I looked at him.

"So?" he said.

"I just think that sometimes it would be nice if you two joined the group. That's all I'm saying," I said. "And maybe get some fresh air."

"We do join the group. Meals. Swimming. Expeditions to the islands. All the evenings with Jorge."

"Okay, you're right. You do join the group."

"And we come upstairs regularly to get cookies." He grinned at me. Cheeky monkey. They'd found a bottomless bowl of Oreos in the lounge, something none of the other mothers knew about. Maybe it was invisible to people over the age of eighteen.

Ben also spent a lot of solitary time while we were motoring at sea, but he chose the back deck of the *Alta* as his refuge. This was a cramped spot with two wicker armchairs, and he was usually the only person sitting there since it was extremely noisy and smelly from the diesel engine right below. He couldn't explain to me in language I could understand why he preferred this spot.

The Galapagos Islands is a group of over fifteen islands in the Pacific Ocean off the coast of Ecuador. They are bisected by the equator, which we crossed a couple of times as we sailed. The first time, we all crowded onto the ship's bridge and watched as the navigation instrument moved to 0000, and then were served a sticky, sweet drink, non-alcoholic for the children and the abstemious. The ritual felt a bit forced to me, contrived just for us Northerners.

The equator is not an arbitrary geographical designation, but it is invisible. It lives in our collective mythology as a romantic destination, although an awful lot of it goes through ocean or uninhabitable terrain. The Galapagos, for example, are barely fit for people. Most of the islands have no fresh water source, nor anything indigenous for people to eat, unless you count the giant tortoises. Not surprisingly, most are uninhabited — and, as a designated UNESCO heritage site, they will remain so.

Every day we had sun and heat and every day we had mist and rain. It was fantastically beautiful. We snorkelled at the base of a cliff and into a grotto where a Galapagos fur seal came to play. Jorge dove with the seal and they swam together in loops, the rest of us watching, legs dangling in the greeny-gloom of the cave. Thomas took over when Jorge surfaced and when the boy came up for air he was laughing. The seal nudged him and down they went again.

The two *pangas*, as they called the Zodiac boats, took us over to the islands for some sightseeing. The sights were all natural: birds, iguanas, giant red crabs, and tortoises. On our first full day we went to Tower Island, where we saw the famous boobies. We saw all three kinds: blue-footed, red-footed, and Nazca. We saw baby boobies, little balls of white fluff perched in a thorny tree. We saw red-footed boobies doing a mating dance. We saw a young blue-footed booby sitting beside a signpost low to the ground. The sign was white with an arrow painted in booby-blue, pointing along the path. This was the only sign we saw on this island and I guess that baby booby found it companionable.

The astonishment was that the wildlife was so tame. Telephoto lenses were unnecessary; we could crouch down and snap a photo from a metre away. For many generations these animals had had nothing to fear from humans and were, therefore, not afraid. We approached, they remained.

I thought of the great blue heron that liked to stand on the end of the canoe dock at the cottage. It would watch me carefully as I inched closer and closer, as slowly as I could, taking forever. I sent it clear and loving vibrations but no matter, once I came within four metres, it flew away. I wished it could see these boobies, calm as can be. Or even the great blue herons on the beach in Florida that will blithely walk a crowded beach and try to steal from a fisherman's pail. Yeats reminded me that the great blues do come to the Galapagos, and he was right. We'd already seen some in Guayaquil, but they weren't the ones that migrate to Muskoka and stand waiting for frogs on the end of our dock.

On the same island we saw more magnificent frigate birds, the males with their huge red neck pouches extended in courtship. They, too, were unafraid, and were so glorious that some of us took far too many photographs.

Yeats said, "Do we really need more than, say, two good photos of one kind of bird? Do we? Do we really, Mom?"

"Some people obviously think so. They can do what they like."

"But it's so dumb. They could be enjoying the birds."

"They are, in their own way. Plus, they're enjoying taking pictures. Some people love to take pictures. It's an art."

"Fifty pictures of the same bird isn't an art form. It's craziness."

I secretly agreed, but Yeats could be so adamant. I didn't want him to grow up to be harshly judgmental, so I tried to temper his rants.

"They're looking for the perfect picture. That's all."

"There's no such thing. Or, every picture is perfect."

I stared at him for a second then went to look at another bird.

Some of the male frigate birds looked like they were suffocating, their neck pouches were so large. They spread their long black wings out to the sides like cormorants on a perch, staying put in spite of our stares.

When we finally tore our eyes away and looked behind us at the view, we saw a cloud of birds flying just off the island's rocky coast. Jorge said they were two kinds of storm petrels: Galapagos and white-rumped. There must have been a couple thousand individuals in that flock, and we watched, enthralled, as they circled and swooped and circled again.

Lauren said, "Why don't they crash into each other?" and some adult began an explanation. But truly, this was one of the mysteries. To be reminded of life's mysteries was a delicious gift and I moved away so as not to hear the scientific explanation. I glanced at Lauren, who was looking perplexed by the account, but I knew she wouldn't have been happy with "It's magic," either.

EVERY DAY JORGE TOOK us out in the *pangas*. One afternoon, near Isabela Island, we donned our rain jackets over our shorts and T-shirts and loaded into the two small boats. We sat up along the high rubber sides, eight to a boat, plus a driver.

It was drizzling, misty in the distance. High cliffs of reddish-yellow stone were the main feature of this side of Isabela. Small caves were dotted here and there in the cliffs, and many ledges were full of perching birds. We saw more blue-footed boobies, gulls, and a kind of tern called the brown noddy. It was love at first sight for me. Like all terns, this one had a small, sleek body and an arrow-straight bill. Its feathers were dark brown with light brown around the head. I don't know why these birds captured my heart; there is no logic to love. As we sat bobbing in our boats, my eyes were glued to the noddies and I had a feeling I had a silly smile on my face. I kept saying to Ben, "Will you look at those birds. Aren't they so beautiful?"

I also have a love of sparrows. A friend of mine once asked why I bothered looking at sparrows, saying, "Aren't they the most boring bird ever?" I was aghast at his lack of knowledge, and then at myself for being such a birding snob. "Clearly," I said, "you don't know about sparrows. How about the white-crowned sparrow with the black and white stripes on its head? Or the white-throated sparrow with the yellow eye patches that sings, *Sweet Canada, Canada, Canada*? Or the song sparrow with its chest stripes and beautiful song?"

He looked at me with chagrin and said, "You mean there's more than one kind of sparrow?"

We continued touring Isabela and saw what looked like prehistoric rock paintings, but they must have been a natural phenomenon. There is no known history of indigenous people in the Galapagos and besides, who would climb all the way up there to carve curlicues in the cliff? These decorated rocks were mesmerizing, in any case, and people snapped photo after photo, despite the rain and terrible light.

Someone saw a spotted eagle ray in the water, and we spent half an hour trying to get a good look at it. The two *pangas* chased and circled the poor creature and the two groups of people took photos of the others trying to take photos of the ray. It never rose completely out of the water, but we saw its "wings" flapping the surface and its form hovering just beneath. It was huge and exotic, mythical.

All the movement and wave action lulled little Fiona to sleep and she dropped against me. I held her up with one arm and clung to Ben with the other while making sure my feet were well planted on the bottom of the boat. Fiona's parents were in the other *panga* and looked over anxiously from time to time. I smiled at them; I wouldn't let her fall into the ocean.

The *panga* drivers signalled to one another and the two boats raced each other back to the *Alta*. By this time, Fiona was wide awake. Jorge told us to crowd up close to the bow to make us go faster. He wanted to win. Ron was sitting right at the bow and he looked quite pleased to have Laurie, Jane, Meredith, and me suddenly piled on top of him. We were laughing so hard we didn't care who won the race, it was just so much fun to be doing something silly in the rain. Then I heard Jorge yell to Fiona that there would be hot chocolate waiting for us on the boat.

On one of our *panga* rides we saw a group of Galapagos penguins sunning themselves on rocks next to some Galapagos sea lions. The Galapagos are the smallest penguins, with an average weight of less than 2.5 kilograms. They are the only penguins with no particular breeding season and have been known to breed up to three times a year. This is in adaptation to an unreliable food source — when food is abundant, they breed more often and sometimes, when food is scarce, they produce no young at all. They are at the mercy of ocean currents as well as weather patterns such as El Niño, all highly variable in the Galapagos.

We watched them slide off the rocks headfirst, like children in a water park, and swim under water. We saw them swimming while we snorkelled. They looked like fat fish, except that they flapped their wings to move themselves through the water. At first, I found it disconcerting to see a bird swimming. One time I saw a common loon swimming at the cottage, but I'd been standing on the dock and it was underwater, distorted by the waves. This time, *I* was underwater too, watching these birds swim past. If I'd thought

about it before I would have been blasé at the prospect of seeing a penguin swim, but in the moment I was astonished. It
took my breath away.

Another day we spent some time on Isabela Island to see
the giant tortoises and the yellow land iguanas. Here we also
saw some of Darwin's finches. Not even Jorge could tell them
apart without spending time comparing them to one another
and to the photos in his guidebook. The differences between
the fifteen varieties were pretty small, mostly to do with size
and shape of beak. We didn't bother trying to identify them,
just checked "Darwin's finch" off our lists and carried on. We
also saw yellow mangrove warblers, small yellow passerines
with rust-coloured faces.

We stopped at Fernandina Island and disembarked from
the *pangas* onto black lava rocks, which were covered in black
marine iguanas and thousands of colourful Sally Lightfoot
crabs. It was very hot in this place and I sensed that some
of the group were restless, but still we paused to watch blue-
footed boobies diving for fish off a rocky promontory. Jorge
told us that they kept their mouths shut until they were under
water, when they scooped up the fish. If they left their mouths
open, the force of the water hitting the backs of their throats
would make them explode. It reminded me of the pelicans
we'd watched diving for fish in Florida, but these boobies
were much more graceful, being smaller and more stream-
lined. They tucked their wings along their bodies and looked
like racing arrows as they plunged into the sea. Five or six
of them dove at once in nearly the same place, then another

three hit the water soon after. It looked like choreographed manoeuvres, a boobie air show.

WE WERE OFF TO Bartholomew Island to watch the sunrise. It was a climb of about half an hour to the top of the island, which is small and rocky. Just about anyone who has looked through photos of the Galapagos would recognize this place, with its rock tower jutting up from the ocean and its perfectly circular bay. A couple of large cruise ships had anchored there. They looked huge next to the *Alta* and we were glad all those people weren't joining us on our sunrise trek.

We saw no birds on Bartholomew. There were no trees, and nothing for animals of any kind to eat except for a few scrubby bushes here and there. It was amazing to us how different these islands were from one another. We had breakfast back on board the boat and set off on a fairly long trip to refuel on another island, Baltra.

Hours later we disembarked on a lovely beach, the first one we'd seen where tourists were allowed to hang out. All the other beaches we'd been to had been protected for the sake of the wildlife. We carried water and juice and beer with us. We wore our swimsuits and brought along a Frisbee and soccer ball. The women sat with bottles of beer at the water's edge, all in a line, and David snapped a photo. We laughed and then posed for him, smiling and hamming it up like beach babes. We were having fun. A game of catch started up in the water with the soccer ball and quickly turned into a team sport complete with goaltenders and a scoreboard.

Ben and I wandered away from this competitive activity and found a couple of birds. Yeats joined us for a while and told us what they were: lava gulls, laughing gulls, and sanderlings. Then he joined the game while Ben and I took a quiet moment to ourselves farther down the beach. It was lovely and peaceful. The water was warm. We were in the tropics.

Ben said, "We could do this. We could take a Caribbean holiday one time."

It was a miracle! Maybe he was developing a travel bug at last.

We wandered back to watch the game, but by then most people had stopped playing. Apparently the ball had a small hole in it, so every time it landed in the ocean, it took on a bit more water, until finally it was too heavy for most people to throw. Yeats, Thomas, and Jorge were the only three left at the end and they played a game of Monkey in the Middle while everyone else had something to drink.

The *Alta* was full of fuel and ready for the long journey around the island of Santa Cruz and into Puerto Ayora. Back on board, most of us showered and got dressed for dinner. Laurie and I were teased for wearing linen trousers with long, loose tops because most of the others were in shorts and T-shirts. My sister and I were a bit too chic.

The grown-ups went up to the top deck for sundowners and the sunset. Fernando brought us popcorn and we lolled about happily after a day of exercise and fun. The sun set promptly at six o'clock, after which we went down into the lounge to hear about the next day's itinerary. The wind had picked up during sunset, and now the waves were starting to rock the boat uncomfortably. I went downstairs to take a Gravol and lie on the bed for a minute.

Then we hit the reef.

The boat made a horrible grinding noise and then pitched to starboard. I sat up. The noise was right underneath me, so I had a pretty good idea right away that we'd hit something.

The boat stopped but made the noise again, several times. That was apparently when the skipper tried to back up, off the reef, to no avail. The boat lurched again, this time to port, and I got off the bed and hurried upstairs.

Everyone was on their feet in the lounge. Jorge was shouting for one person per cabin to go downstairs and fetch the life jackets and their passports. I looked across the room at Yeats who mouthed, "It's okay." I guess I looked worried. I *was* worried. I wanted Yeats and Ben right beside me, but there was no chance of that.

I turned around and went back down the staircase, since I was closest. People followed me — Tom, I think, and Stephen and Andy. I went back into our cabin and grabbed my little knapsack. I opened the top drawer of the bedside table and took out the passports, the envelope of cash, and my reading glasses, and stuffed them into the pack. If I'd opened the next drawer down, I would have taken my journal, too, the loss of which I've rued ever since. And if I'd stopped for ten seconds to rifle through what I'd grabbed, I'd have realized I had only Ben and Yeats's passports, not my own.

The whole time, the boat was pitching back and forth, the wind was howling, and the waves were crashing against both the boat and the reef. Back upstairs I tossed a life jacket to Ben, who was still on the other side of the room. I didn't see Yeats—he'd gone down with Thomas to fetch their life jackets along with those of the little girls. I put mine on and tried to figure out what we were all to do.

Someone called out, "Into the Zodiacs! We're getting in the Zodiacs! Everyone on the back deck!"

I stepped out the starboard door onto the narrow walkway that went from bow to stern. We lurched violently to starboard, then to port. There were people all around but in that moment, the only person I saw was Monica, one of the crew members. In the same instant that I noticed she wasn't wearing a life jacket, I saw, beyond her, huge waves rolling in towards the boat. The waves were illuminated in the ship's lights, faint and ghostly against the black sky.

I groaned aloud and said, "Oh. My. God." I was frozen.

Monica put a hand on my arm and said, "It's okay. It's going to be okay."

That one second of fear stretched for an eternity, turned me inside out, unbuckled me from my life. Then Tom was pushing past me with seven-year-old Fiona in front and Barb right behind. His uncharacteristic aggression snapped me back into myself. I followed them, but that one split second was lodged inside me now. It was an instant that I would flash back to again and again in the weeks to come.

People were shouting instructions and one another's

names and it was all action. We had to time our individual exits from the boat perfectly. We had to let go of the starboard railing and slide down the sea-drenched deck, one at a time, to the other side, where two crew members hoisted us onto the railing and helped us time our jump into the Zodiacs.

Carlos, who was driving one of the Zodiacs, timed it so that the waves and the tipping boat were aligned and we all made the jump safely. We were grabbed by someone and made to sit down anywhere there was room, preferably on the bottom of the boat to keep from falling out.

Jorge, who was driving the second Zodiac, motored in to collect the remaining passengers and crew. Ben was among them, and I watched as he slipped on the deck and crashed into the railing. I was relieved when he jumped successfully into the waiting *panga*. Jorge collected Andy and Ron, too, and brought them over to our boat. As Ben, Andy, and Ron scrambled into our Zodiac, Ron's biggest worry was that his shorts were falling off (which they were). This supplied the two little girls with hours of amusement over the next few days. All of us except Stephen and most of the crew were now in one little rubber boat.

Ben told me later that after I'd left the lounge to go outside, the boat had made a particularly bad pitch (my scary wave) and Meredith ended up on the floor, clinging to the table. She couldn't get up because every time she tried, the boat pitched again and the table slid. Ben tried to help her up but fell and became stuck, both arms stretched in opposite directions. (When he fell, he broke his baby toe, but he didn't say anything about it until hours later, when we were alone in our hotel room and he was telling me all of this.) Meredith was on the edge of panic, and it was all Ben could do to try to calm her down while extricating himself from the furniture.

Yeats would tell me about it later, too. As soon as he walked into the lounge, he said, he saw Ben and Meredith sitting on the floor, unable to get up. So Yeats stepped over to Ben, stuck out his hand, and said, "Come on, Dad, it's time to get out of here." That must have been the only time that Yeats had ever called Ben "Dad." Yeats hauled Ben up, who then hauled Meredith up and then they left the lounge for the boats.

We needed to keep the *panga* away from the reef, which could puncture the boat's rubber hull, but the waves kept pushing us back. I was sitting near the stern, facing forwards. We were all crammed in together—fifteen of us plus Carlos—in an eight-person boat. Some people had to sit up on the rounded sides and brace themselves every time a wave came.

Then the motor conked out. Tom and Andy grabbed paddles and started paddling furiously to keep us off the reef. Carlos tried to restart the engine but it flooded. People were shouting instructions. Someone scrambled to the back of the boat to lend a hand. We'd all flooded outboard motors in Muskoka and got them going again, but never under such stressful circumstances. Still, it helped that all of us had spent our lives in and around boats. We had a second sense about boats and water and no one panicked.

I wasn't ready, though, for the sight of the final wave. It was as though the wind had been building up and up and up until finally it created what it had been striving toward the whole time. This wave must have been fifteen feet high. It was a wall of water coming right for us, and the *Alta* beyond. I saw it coming, but didn't say a word. There was no time.

Our little boat rode it out. We didn't tip. We just went up and over the other side, like in a ride at an amusement park. Everyone gasped, though, and turned to watch it hit the *Alta*. The wave crashed against the ship, flooding its uppermost deck and tipping it further over onto the reef. This time it stayed tipped.

After that the ocean was calm. The wind was gone. No more storm, just like that: from one moment to the next.

We could see lights from shore and lots of anchored yachts, but we were still a ways out there and unsure about any rescue. We still didn't know why this had happened and whether we'd get any of our stuff off the *Alta*. We also couldn't see the other *panga*, so we didn't know where Jorge was with the crew, or even whether Stephen was safely off the ship. Jane was frantic and blew incessantly on the whistle attached to her life jacket.

Once the engine was fixed we motored slowly in to shore. We were bedraggled and mystified, wet, tired, and worried. We went past yachts where people were eating their dinners. They sat at tables lit with candles, drinking wine and laughing. They had no idea that this little *panga* filled with stunned tourists was moving among them. Evidently, no mayday message had been sent out.

It turned out that Jorge had deposited Stephen and some of the crew on an isthmus and then gone back to look for the other crew members. Jorge had his cell phone with him and called his friend, Julian, who ran the Hotel Solymar, telling him to pick us up at the wharf and to find us clothes and give us anything we wanted. The owners of the *Alta* would pay.

Julian, his wife, and all his staff were wonderful. They picked us up and brought us back to a lovely hotel with a terrace overlooking the water. We were all at least slightly in shock and most of the adults wanted a drink.

Andy said, "Do you have a good Scotch?"

Julian said, "I do. Do you want that on the rocks?"

"On the what?" Laurie said, and after a second or two, we all laughed. It was a relief to laugh. Julian laughed, too, and fetched a bottle of his best Scotch. No one had it on ice.

They brought pizza but few of us could eat. I think the kids ate. All I'd had since lunch was some popcorn, a gin and tonic, two Gravol, and a couple of ounces of Scotch. I forced down a few bites.

Stephen and Jorge appeared on the terrace and Jane gave a shriek.

Eventually, we learned that the captain hadn't been driving the boat as we approached Puerto Ayora. The second mate was driving and the captain was attending to accounts. The reef was supposed to have two lighthouses on it, but only one was working. Plus, the waves had definitely been getting bigger and bigger. All of these factors combined to cause the accident. Once the second mate realized the boat was on the reef, he put the engine in reverse and tried to back it up, but it was too late.

Ecuador takes Galapagos' UNESCO designation very seriously. Visitors are not allowed to bring animals or plants or even foodstuffs that might contaminate the ecosystem. People are supposed to decontaminate their shoes after walking on one island and before they walk on another, because each island represents a different ecological microcosm. There are pages and pages of rules. But here was a boat, full of fuel, stuck on a precious, sensitive reef, causing who knows how much damage. We were all sick at heart.

Jorge went back out to the boat late that night. He scaled it like a monkey, according to David — who went along but didn't try to enter the *Alta* himself. Jorge's goal was to retrieve Rón's medications, which he needed for his blood pressure and his heart. The Coast Guard had ordered everyone off the boat, including the captain, who'd been planning to stay at least overnight to guard against looters. But he'd obeyed the order and the Coast Guard had posted no one on guard duty, so Jorge took a calculated risk and went into the boat on his own.

He gave us a full report when they returned. The ship was full of water, especially the rooms on the downward side. It felt stable on the reef, but he suspected that was only because the sea was calm and there was no wind. He'd found Ron's travel case, but not his and Barb's passports. We'd given him a list of things to retrieve if possible, including my passport and those of Tom, Ron, Barb, and Fiona. But there was too much water, and he knew that if he stayed too long, the Coast Guard would catch him.

But he had Ron's medications and Jorge was now truly our hero. He had lost everything himself. His passport, all his camera gear — including videos of an underwater shoot he'd just completed in the Arctic — his computer. Everything was under water and he would have to start over again.

The next day Jorge said to Yeats, "This morning I couldn't figure out why my arms were so sore. It wasn't that much work scaling the boat. But then I remembered our game of Monkey in the Middle with that heavy ball!"

They had a good laugh together over that, and it turned out to be one of Yeats's favourite memories of the trip.

BEN AND I WERE lying in bed on our second morning in the Hotel Solymar on Santa Cruz, our final morning in the Galapagos. I'd been crying a bit but he held me and I stopped.

He said, "The Sufis say that all you really have in life is what you can take with you from a shipwreck." I looked into his eyes. We had one another. He said, "I'm not too good with the emotional stuff," meaning that he wasn't going to cry. I knew Ben well enough to realize that any toughness he showed on the outside masked a deeply caring and loving heart inside. He held me closer and whispered, "I love you, Lynn. Let's go home now."

The airport was on Baltra, just off the coast of Santa Cruz. We took a bus across Santa Cruz to a small marina where we boarded one last boat. This boat was flat-bottomed and way overloaded with passengers, none of whom wore a life jacket. We were crammed in there like sardines. It was a really short trip—maybe ten minutes—and the day was calm. But we stole glances at each other as we were waiting to leave the pier, most of us holding onto straps from the ceiling, like in the subway.

Thomas said, "This is fun! Another boat!"

Fiona said, "What if we shipwreck?"

"We aren't going to shipwreck," four or five of us said at once. Other passengers looked at us but didn't say anything.

Ben said, "You'll have some stories for your friends."

Fiona nodded and looked up at him with her huge green eyes. She whispered, "But what if we *do* shipwreck?"

Ben shook his head and said, "We won't. Look. We're here already."

The boat pulled up to the wharf and we jostled our way off.

The flight was to Guayaquil, from where we were supposed to fly home in a couple of days. But those of us without passports had to stay on the plane and fly to Quito, where the Canadian embassy was located. We'd been in touch by phone, giving them our names and other pertinent information, and they were ready to issue us letters of transit. We had to be there in person to receive the documents.

Ben and I sat next to one another on the flight to Guayaquil. He and Yeats would disembark when we arrived there, while I went on with the others to Quito. I said, "If it takes too long in Quito, you and Yeats are going straight home anyway, right?"

"No. We'll wait for you. Are you crazy?"

"No, you need to get home. Yeats has to go to school. You have that big event. You have to go."

"No, we don't. We can't just leave you here."

"I won't be alone." I gestured to the others who had to get travel documents too. Tom, Fiona, Ron, and both Barbs were all coming to Quito, along with Andy, who had his passport but wanted to accompany his parents.

"Nuh-uh, no way. We're not flying home without you."

I stopped arguing but I was frustrated. I'd travelled all over the world and knew how to get home on my own. But when the plane landed in Guayaquil and everyone stood up to say goodbye, the fact of the separation, even one so brief, hit me. Ben and Yeats gave me a hug and started moving down the aisle. As I watched them disappear off the plane, it felt like someone was cutting off a part of me; it was a physical wrenching.

I lost my senses. I sat back down and cried. I gulped for air and sobbed, and within fifteen seconds my face was soaking wet. We'd just been through this traumatic experience together and now I had to say goodbye to them? I didn't know how I was ever going to pull myself together.

Tom moved over and sat beside me. He was an emergency room doctor and knew how to deal with people who were in shock. He calmed me down. He talked to me the entire flight to Quito and helped restore me to my right mind without once referring to my emotional reaction. I knew what he was doing as he was doing it, but it worked anyway and I am eternally grateful.

It turned out that Andy's passport was waterlogged and the embassy staff told him he wouldn't be able to use it, so he needed new documents too. And his wasn't the only one — practically everyone else in our group ended up in Quito by the next morning, trading their waterlogged documents for papers saying they could go home. Only Ben, Yeats, Stephen, and Jane had useable passports.

The first batch of us received our letters and we flew back to Guayaquil the next day. Ben and the others were waiting for us in the airport, and I cried all over again. It felt like weeks, instead of one long night, since I'd last seen them.

EIGHT

WE ARRIVED HOME IN Toronto on Sunday morning. Thankfully there was no snow on the ground or in the air, because we were in flip-flops and I was the only one wearing pants, linen though they were. Ben and Yeats, in shorts and T-shirts, thought the whole thing was pretty funny and I was so worn out I didn't care. It was awfully nice not to have any baggage to wait for, but I was disappointed that I had to turn in my letter of transit with its terrible photo of me. It would have made a good souvenir.

That afternoon Ben took Yeats shopping to buy shoes for school, which started the next day. Yeats only ever had one pair of shoes at a time; consumerism was low on his list of priorities. According to him, the less stuff he had, the better, with the possible exception of books.

The next day I called the school and spoke to David Reed, Yeats' mentor. I told him about the shipwreck and asked if he'd keep an eye on Yeats. I was worried that this incident might have stirred up the emotions that Yeats felt when Mr. Dewees killed himself only five months before. I knew it had stirred up all kinds of things in me: fears, mostly.

I said, "I have no idea if he'll crash the way he did when David Dewees died, but I want to know someone is watching out for him."

"Coffee House is coming up," David said. Coffee House was the evening event created by the poetry club for students and teachers to entertain one another with poetry and song. "I'll be working closely with Yeats over the next couple of weeks anyway. How is he at home?"

"Mostly the same as usual. Won't talk to me, then does. Hates school, but does his work. Happy one moment, surly the next."

"In other words, a pretty typical teen."

"I guess."

"You need to remember, you're the mother. Kids feel safe with the mother and will drop all their fears and anxieties at your feet. If he's feeling vulnerable, he'll show it at home, not at school with us. Did you say, by the way, that you lost your own passport but not the others'?"

"Yes. I grabbed Ben and Yeats's passports and missed my own. I had to go to Quito without them."

"You're the mother, always taking care of everyone else first." He'd nailed it; an English teacher catching the symbolism.

David called me the next day and said he'd spoken with most of Yeats's teachers and told them that I was concerned and that they should please call me if they noticed anything amiss. I thanked him and felt a twinge of guilt, knowing that Yeats would probably be mad at me for going behind his back like this. But he was still a child, just sixteen, and if he really was fine (as he said he was), then he didn't need to feel self-conscious knowing adults were looking out for him. None of the teachers called me. He really *was* fine.

The next day, Yeats came home from school with two great projects. Mr. Reed had asked him to put together a CD of his favourite songs to play while people were arriving for Coffee House. And his English teacher had asked him to make a list of his ten favourite poems for the class to study in the upcoming weeks. I didn't know if these men would have asked Yeats to do these things if I hadn't made that call to the school. Maybe they would have. But I appreciated it anyway, because I saw the joy on Yeats's face when he was telling me about these projects.

We talked about which poems to include. I said, "How about 'The Cinnamon Peeler' by Michael Ondaatje?" and went to the shelf to find the book.

He said, "You don't need to read it out. It's a good one, though, really beautiful." He put it on the list.

"And what about that one about the cloths of heaven?" I asked expectantly. Yeats knew it was my favourite W. B. Yeats poem.

He laughed at me and said, "Okay, that one, too. It's nice and short."

I scanned the shelves for Ben's old *Representative Poetry*, and got down the dusty and slightly mouldy-smelling volume. Twelve-page poems by Pope, twenty-page poems by Keats. I thought not. Far more interesting in this book were the little pieces of paper Ben had stuck into it over the years. There were old ticket stubs from concerts — the Kinks, the Eagles — small bookmarks from novels published in the 1970s, and even a flyer promoting the Lotos Eaters, the band Ben sang in when he was younger.

So we went on with life, work, school. In a typical week, Ben worked at least three nights, as well as five or six days in the shop. We had book launches in the store in the evenings or we sold books at off-site events, and sometimes I worked at those functions too. We were back to the pace of the previous fall. Some weeks, Ben had an event every night. He was really tired. We were all uncharacteristically tired after the trip, trying to recalibrate.

Some days I found myself pussy-footing around Ben. He was so crabby. I was afraid to interrupt him to ask for help or to fix a problem. It was not that I was afraid he'd explode at me, but that he'd give me the silent treatment or glare at me like I should already know everything.

Simone said, "What's eating him?"

I sighed and said, "He's sore somewhere. Probably his feet, that broken toe, or his knees, or just his legs in general. He doesn't get enough sleep and he doesn't eat properly. All the same old things."

"Huh. Maybe he needs a real holiday."

"Maybe he needs not to work five double-shifts every week."

Plus, I thought to myself, *maybe we need more time alone together.* He gave me tight little kisses goodbye, which made me feel like crap. Simone saw the look on my face and said, "It'll be okay. He'll work this out like he always does, you'll see." She came over and rubbed my back.

But it wasn't just Ben. I was crabby, too. I called my friend Chris in Halifax and I cried a bit.

"Take care of yourself, Lynnie," she said. "Can you do something nice? Go out for dinner with a girlfriend or maybe go away for a weekend? Don't take care of everyone else and leave yourself for last." She would know, with three children of her own. "Besides," she joked, "we're about to turn fifty. It's time to have a little bit of fun."

ONLY A MONTH AFTER we returned from the Galapagos, I was already planning two trips: a birding expedition to Pelee Island for the May bird migration and another in the summer to visit BC, ostensibly to scout out universities for Yeats but also to bird-watch and see friends. My flashbacks to the shipwreck were becoming less frequent; Ben and Yeats claimed to have no flashbacks at all, ever.

We were all back to our regular routines, school and work, but something was out of kilter for me. My teeth were sore. Did I need a root canal? Then I noticed I was clenching my jaw. Whenever I stopped to think about it, I found that my jaw was firmly clenched.

I was at a café downtown, sitting with a cappuccino and watching people go by, something I used to do all the time but never did anymore. It felt good to relax, but my jaw was still clenched. I unclenched it. I sipped my coffee and had to unclench my jaw again.

I thought it was time for a little self-examination. I sat there and said out loud (in my head), *What on earth has happened to make me so persistently anxious?* I thought back over the last days and weeks, and bumped up against the shipwreck and its stressful aftermath. Of course! Maybe it should have been obvious, this residual anxiety, but to me, it wasn't. I'd been going to my Wednesday-morning writing group and I'd written about what happened on the trip, but not about my feelings or anxieties. Nor had I written about them in my daily journal. It was like they were stuck: in my body, in my jaw. Now I recognized the experience of the shipwreck for the power it still had over me, and I have to say I was relieved I didn't need a root canal.

I called a girlfriend who was a yoga instructor and she said, "We hold everything in our bodies." I remembered that from my yoga days, too. Our bodies hold the keys to our emotions, if we only know how to find the door. So now that I'd found the door, how did I open it?

Someone suggested therapy. Someone else suggested homeopathy. Another friend said lots of wine might be good (she wasn't joking) and my doctor recommended exercise (which was her advice for everything psychological). I appreciated the advice, but had to find something that would fit into my daily life. I opted for massage with cranial-sacral therapy, once a month, as well as long walks with my friend Anne, and wine with friends on a regular basis. And bird-watching, which turned out to be a perfect choice.

The clenching abated and the flashbacks stopped, but something was left behind. A shadow of disquiet followed me around and when I thought about travelling, it enveloped me.

BEFORE GOING TO PELEE Island, people asked if I was afraid of the ferry ride, the one-and-a-half-hour crossing of Lake Erie. I knew they were asking because of the Galapagos affair, and most people were asking partly in jest. No one had died, and so the shipwreck had become a great joke.

I looked at the possibility of fearing this crossing, and the one coming up in the summer from Vancouver to Victoria, and all the boat rides all summer long in Muskoka. I thought about the possibility of fearing the boats, the water, another shipwreck. I knew now, in a different kind of way than I had before, that freak accidents could happen to ordinary people, and that knowledge was in my body. My awareness had shifted. When we boarded the ferry, I looked for the exits; I looked for the life jacket stations, the muster stations. I prepared myself in a way I'd never thought to before. Yet this shift in awareness felt, to me, more practical than fearful.

Where I was sensing the shadow, though, was in a lack of joy. I was not having those fleeting joyful moments I usually had when contemplating a trip. Usually I loved setting out for somewhere I'd never been and felt an expansiveness in my chest just thinking about it for weeks in advance. This time, that shadow filled the space instead.

Once I'd driven the car onto the ferry to Pelee Island, Yeats and I walked out on deck but a cold, fierce wind was blowing, so we went back inside.

I said, "Let's sit in the canteen and play cards."

Yeats said, "Okay, let's play Rummy."

The boat tipped and rocked in the waves and every once in a while we looked up from our game.

I said, "Remember those waves?"

"Don't think about it, Mom. We don't need to worry."

"You're right." We laughed a bit and I said, "But remember that really big wave, the one that tipped the boat right over? We were all in the *panga* and this giant wall of a wave came along and then that was it."

"Yeah, that was the last wave."

"It's kind of amazing that no one was sick."

"There was no time to be sick. Think about it. It all happened so fast—the crash, getting into the *pangas*. It was chaos."

"But not really chaos. No one panicked."

"Right."

"You were especially calm. Like now. Here you are, calming down your momma before she even gets jumpy."

While I felt comforted by Yeats, I still didn't have that old carefree feeling I was used to having when my son and I were on the road. I was waiting for something to uncloud my heart.

Most of my friends had either never heard of Pelee Island or had some vague idea that it was a bird migration route. When I pushed them, though, it became clear they were thinking of Point Pelee, on the mainland, rather than the island itself. When I told them what I'd learned about it—that it was closer to the U.S. than to Canada, that since 1860 its farmers had been growing grapes for wine, that it had great beaches and gorgeous sunrises—they said, "Really? Why have I never heard of it?" I told them I had no idea.

The island is the permanent residence of about three hundred people, and another 1,200 or more cottage there every summer. It is the southernmost populated part of Canada and tends to have milder weather than the rest of the country. It is also part of the Carolinian forest, and the landscape is as flat as a pancake.

We arrived mid-morning, settled into our inn, then drove to a place marked "Fish Point" on the map. A couple of cars were parked at the trailhead, and on our walk through the woods we saw very few people. The whole place felt under-populated.

It was sunny but still windy and cool, so I wore nylon rain pants over my trousers. We weren't even twenty metres into the forest before Yeats (who was wearing shorts) turned around and said, "Mom, your pants are driving me crazy. They're too loud."

"What? Too loud? I need them to keep me warm."

"Well, they're too loud. Listen to them."

We walked a bit farther. I was thinking that I needed these rain pants to keep me warm and I was irritated by Yeats's comment since he rarely felt cold. He didn't understand. But then I stopped this internal chatter and listened for a bit and finally heard what he was hearing. They were really annoying.

"Okay, you're right. I'm going to take them off." I took off the offending pants and stuffed them in my backpack.

In the forest on the way to the beach we saw all kinds of warblers, including our first sighting of the Cape May warbler. This beautiful yellow bird has black stripes on its chest, an olive back, and red patches on its face. It is named for Cape May, New Jersey, where it was first described. But after that first sighting, it wasn't seen in Cape May for another hundred years. It has an unusual tongue — curled and semi-tubular — which it uses to collect nectar during its winter sojourns in the West Indies.

We also saw a blue-grey gnatcatcher and a wood thrush. Both of these birds were rooting around in a swampy area off the path and it took a great deal of time and patience for us to get a positive ID on them. The thrush, especially, seemed determined to elude us, but we had time to spare. We had nothing but time, really. When there was no rush and no schedule, time expanded, and I felt my heart expand, too. This day, this thrush, everything in that moment, was miraculous.

The blue-grey gnatcatcher is a tiny bird, ten to eleven centimetres in length, smaller than the wren. It is blue-grey all over, except for a white bit under its tail, which it constantly flicks to stir up insects. It is the only migratory gnatcatcher and is seldom seen; we were very happy to spot it here, where we could watch it undisturbed as it flitted from branch to branch.

The wood thrush was a big deal for Yeats. We saw hermit thrushes every spring in our back garden, but this was our first sighting of their cousin. In silhouette it looks like a scaled-down American robin, but its colouring is different: cinnamon back and brown-and-white spotted chest. It is far shyer than the robin and doesn't winter over in southern Canada the way the robin does. Instead it flies to Central America and spends those cold months in tropical forests.

We took our time on the path, finding white-crowned sparrows, mourning warblers, and the ubiquitous chickadees, and by the time we got to the shore the wind had really picked up.

We stood on a deserted sand spit and looked through our binoculars at all the birds congregated at its tip. Right at the end were about a hundred gulls (ring-billed, herring, great black-backed) and between them and us were at least as many black-bellied plovers. This was a new species for us, so we were thrilled. Mixed among the plovers were other shorebirds and we spent a few happy minutes identifying ruddy turnstones, semipalmated plovers, dunlins, and short-billed dowitchers.

As we walked slowly down the spit, the plovers grew restless. They shifted slightly away from us and kept turning their heads until suddenly, as if at some hidden signal, they all took off into the sky. They split into two groups and flew as beautiful, synchronized flocks, turning and shining in the sun. They flew out over the water then turned and swooped and turned again, silver backs flashing, signalling.

This plover sky ballet—elegant, fast, spiral—made Yeats and I stand still, electrified. I felt my inner shadow lifting in one great rush as they flew. That shipwreck had shut me down and these plovers were beginning to open me up again, lightening my heart. For the thirty seconds of their magnificent flight, I was filled with joy; I felt it bursting from my belly.

I saw that joy on Yeats's face too and once the birds landed on the sand again I whispered, "This whole weekend, every minute of it, was worth it just for that."

He said—well, he didn't say anything. He nodded and then raised his binoculars to look at the shorebirds once more.

I said, "Let's wait and see if they do that again."

WE LUNCHED IN OUR room and decided to forsake the car for the afternoon, walking instead down the road next to the inn. As we left the porch, the first thing we saw was a blue-headed vireo. It was feeding in young trees next to our room and Yeats, of course, spotted it as soon as we stepped outside.

This bird is a small passerine with a blue-grey head and distinctive white wing bars on an olive background. It has obvious white spectacles about its eyes and is a common migrant, but this was the first time we'd seen it.

A road ran parallel to the lake next to the inn, a long,

straight road completely devoid of cars or people. Large deciduous trees overhung this road, oak and chestnut, and possibly
hickory trees, too, but we weren't sure. The trees were full of
gorgeous birds — indigo buntings and rose-breasted gros-
beaks and all kinds of warblers — and smelled lush in a way I
imagined the forests of South Carolina smelling. I wasn't sure
why, since I'd never been to South Carolina. It must have been
the name "Carolinian" playing with my mind, or all those
books I'd read set in the southern United States.

The greenery soon gave way to the Stone Road Alvar
Reserve. An "alvar" is a limestone plain that can withstand
extremes of drought and flood. The alvar on Pelee Island is
the only one in Ontario and is home to more than fifty rare
plant species, making it an important conservation area.
Every fencepost had a flycatcher sitting on it, and we watched
a turkey vulture pulling away at something in a field. We'd
only ever seen these vultures high up in the sky, so we took
some time to enjoy it on the ground, gazing through our binoculars as it ate its carrion lunch.

The road became a grassy path through scrubby bushes
and the grass soon turned to swamp. We decided to go back,
but I really wanted to sit by the lake for a while and rest. I
surprised Yeats by suggesting we tramp through someone's
property down to the shore. I don't think we'd ever tres-
passed before and I knew he was uncomfortable with it, but
we went anyway. No one stopped us and we found the shore
composed of large, flat stones. I flopped down and he did, too,
though somewhat reluctantly.

"What will we say if someone comes out?" he asked.

"I don't know. It doesn't matter." I opened one eye and looked at him. "It really doesn't matter."

The stones were warm and smooth. The lake lapped against them and there was a warm breeze. Yeats spotted some huge fish swimming just off the edge of our resting place and seagulls flew by. It was very peaceful. I wanted to stay and maybe nap on this comfortable rock, but Yeats was restless and so after twenty minutes we walked on.

That night I read for far too long. I was reading Kathleen Winter's new book, *Annabel*. It was so good that I read long after Yeats had fallen asleep and way past the time when I, too, should have been asleep, considering we had a very early start the next day. But sometimes reading comes first and it felt delicious to hunker down in bed with a compelling story.

THE NEXT MORNING WE rose at 5:30 to watch the sunrise. We put on as many layers as we could and walked the one block to the beach. It was cold and pre-dawn grey, and we were the only people out.

"Where do you think it's going to come up?" I asked.

"Maybe over there." Yeats pointed in an easterly direction as I perched on a boulder.

"But where exactly?"

He gave me a look that said, *Not this game, I'm too tired*. But the truth was, we both enjoyed the early morning and had no trouble passing the time before sunrise in companionable contemplation.

Seagulls flew past, calling; a great blue heron flew past, silent, its long legs streaming out behind. We waited for the first orange gleam to break the lake's horizon, eyes scanning the cloudless sky to find it. Grey turning to pink and blue.

"There it is," Yeats said quietly, motioning roughly to where he'd pointed to before.

A tiny, flaming gem perched on the edge of the water and a second later it exploded into a dazzling orange light, growing bigger and bigger and, in less than a minute, it was the sun. I sighed in satisfaction at this perfectly ordinary start to another day on earth. Gratitude flooded me, tears welled up in my eyes, and for a split second I saw the same feeling mirrored on Yeats's face.

He said, "Are we going to go birdwatching before breakfast?"

The inn didn't serve breakfast until 7:30, way late for us birders, and there was nowhere to buy a muffin and a cup of coffee. So we decided to check out the other end of the island, where the map indicated there was an old lighthouse.

Yeats referred to that place later as the "Creepy Blackbird Forest" because that's exactly what it was. It was one of those places the forest has reclaimed after being domesticated. This forest was spindly and messy, overgrown with raspberry and blackberry canes, with sumac, and with straggly willows. While it could still be called a forest, because there were some large trees, it could also be considered a swamp since part of the ground had sunk. Someone had cut trails for birdwatchers, but these trails doubled back on themselves and we spent two hours walking in circles, every once in a while coming out to the lake and spotting the crumbly lighthouse on the point.

All the while, the trill of red-winged blackbirds, hundreds of them, accosted us. It was as though someone had stuffed these woods with mechanical red-winged blackbirds and wound them all up to sing continuously. It could drive a person mad.

It was a huge relief when the woods finally ejected us onto the road and we made our way back to the car. That was one place we'd never go again.

I WAS HAPPY FOR my big breakfast — eggs, toast, fruit, and homemade banana bread — and a couple of cups of coffee. I knew I'd have to pee in the woods later on, and hoped that when I did, I wouldn't have to wait too long to find a secluded spot. With luck, there wouldn't be too many other people in the woods.

Yeats never had to pee; he could hold it all day if he had to. He said it was because of his long hair — not an obvious physiological symbiosis for most people. But when he was younger he'd had a couple of embarrassing episodes in men's washrooms, where the other guys in there thought he was a girl. Nothing sinister, just comments along the line of, "This isn't the ladies'." Ever since, he'd refused to use public toilets, even at school, and so developed a strong bladder.

We got in the car and drove around the island, looking for places to bird-watch. We found an old graveyard
surrounded by tall bushes, which seemed promising, so we
parked and wandered around. We spent a few minutes reading headstones, silently reflecting on the lives of people long
dead. People who lived in a very remote area.

Then Yeats saw a great crested flycatcher up in a tree and
we switched gears back to birdwatching. This was my first
good sighting of the species. It's about twenty centimetres
long, slim-looking, and has a yellow belly with a grey breast
and olive back. When agitated, it lifts the large brown crest
on top of its head, the same way a blue jay does. This one sat
preening, letting us get a good, long look.

Then, in the tall bushes, warblers: yellow-rumped, yellow, black-throated green, chestnut-sided. These bushes,
both to see and to hear, were *alive* with warblers, shimmer-
ing with them. I thought for perhaps the hundredth time that
"warbler" was the perfect way to describe these birds that
sing such musical songs, each species with its different tune
and pitch. Yeats wrote down their names and I stood still in
that bird-filled morning.

We drove around some more and stopped by a farmer's
field. Killdeer were scratching around for grubs. Yeats saw
them right away but, as usual, it took my eyes longer to adjust.
Killdeer blend right in with a fallow field and even though
these were moving, I couldn't see them—until suddenly I
did. "Oh yeah, there they are!" The sharp thrill of seeing
them reminded me of childhood happiness, gifts under the

Christmas tree, perhaps, a kind of euphoria we adults manage to shut out most of the time. This is why I bird-watch, to recapture what it's like to live in this moment, right now.

Pelee Island was a very sleepy place. There seemed to be exactly one shop — a small co-op with limited supplies: bottled water, pop, chips, candy. There was a restaurant at the winery and a few B&Bs. There were some burger spots and ice cream parlours, too, but they were shut for the season. I realized partway through our stay that I saw no one talking on cell phones. I asked Sandra, the woman who ran our inn, about that. She said the reception was spotty and besides, most people came to Pelee Island to get away from things like pesky cell phones.

Sandra told me that she came to Pelee the year before for a weekend with some girlfriends. She wasn't a birder; she and her friends just needed some time off and thought Pelee Island looked out-of-the-way. During that weekend, she toured an inn that was for sale and fell in love with it (and the island). She bought the inn. She said she went home to her husband and children and said, "Guess what I did this weekend? I bought an inn! On Pelee Island!" I tried to imagine doing this myself and decided I must be awfully risk-averse.

The inn needed a lot of work and she was getting it done. Clearly she loved this place and this life. Her dream had always been to own a B&B and now she had it. I hoped part of her dream involved a certain amount of isolation.

Yeats loved the Wandering Pheasant Inn. He loved our huge room with the mismatched antique furniture and the creaky screened-in porch. I liked all the mismatched china in the breakfast room. Sandra was putting in a new deck around the main building, which would be lovely on hot summer days.

We drove down the main street and saw a museum with an OPEN sign out front. The museum had displays about the geology of Pelee, its flora and fauna, its birds and their migrations, as well as information about farming and fishing, the First Nations presence before European settlement, and the European settlers themselves. Someone had put a lot of effort into this little museum and we spent an hour or so wandering around it.

We listened to a man tell the museum attendant that he lost all his honeybees over the winter and would have to start afresh. He said there were no more honeybees on Pelee at all, a grim state of affairs. The attendant was wearing a Nature Conservancy of Canada shirt and I asked him about his affiliation with the organization. He was a member, being a serious birder. He told me about the events they had there with authors and birders, and had I ever heard of Graeme Gibson? I told him I was a bookseller and yes, I knew Graeme and I knew his books. *The Bedside Book of Birds* is a rare treat of a book, a work of art and a meditation on life in the wild. A bookseller's life follows her everywhere.

He told us where to find Graeme's son, who had a bird-tagging project near Fish Point at the southwestern end of the island. He looked at his watch and said maybe we'd catch them, maybe we wouldn't. They usually wrapped up around 11 a.m. and it was already 10:45, but if we hurried...

There was no traffic on the island and we zipped down the road and parked the car just outside the trailhead to Fish Point. We found the nearly invisible trail going off into the woods. Other people were there, too, also looking for the project. They looked at our running shoes but didn't say anything. I looked at their rubber boots.

We went a ways into the forest, which then became a bog. Pretty soon we would have to decide whether or not to turn back. We couldn't see anything up ahead. The forest was sparse with trees, but oddly dense. It was the kind of forest you'd get lost in in ten seconds flat because everywhere in it looked exactly the same.

The museum attendant had told us that early in the mornings, the nets went up to catch songbirds. The birds were then gently removed and some were banded or fitted with transmitters. Then the birds were released, and at eleven o'clock, the nets came down. We didn't see anyone and our feet were quickly soaked, so we turned back.

We went back to the woods leading out to Fish Point and had another look around. We saw a lot of the same birds as on the day before, but not as many, possibly because it was closer to noon, the warmest part of the day.

When we walked on the forest path, Yeats went first. If I went first, I walked too quickly. We missed things. Yeats would fall behind while I worked up a pace, a rhythm more attuned to hiking than birdwatching. It wouldn't be long before he was yelling at me to slow down and then, inevitably, he'd take the lead.

"Mom, you're going too fast!" Oh, yeah, we were bird-watching. What had I already missed?

Yeats thought he heard a wren, so we stopped and sur-veyed the forest. We spotted it through our binoculars, about a hundred metres away, hopping around on some dead branches.

A man wandered up beside us and said, "What is it?"

Yeats said, "A wren, a house wren."

The man raised his huge telephoto lens and after a few seconds, he said, "A Carolina wren, I'd say."

"Well, it's kind of small and there's no white stripe down its face," Yeats said.

"Hmph. I still think it's a Carolina." He looked at Yeats and I imagined what he was thinking: how can this kid know the difference between the house wren and the Carolina wren? The man didn't know that this kid had memorized the bird book long ago, and I didn't tell him. I was the silent witness.

The wren sang its song and Yeats said, "There. It's defi-nitely a house wren."

The man said "Hmph" again and moved on down the trail.

Anger swelled up in my throat. The man could at least have acknowledged Yeats's opinion, engaged in a conversa-tion about the differences between the wrens, maybe admit-ted that the boy *could* be right. The anger startled me, then bothered me, and I dropped it. Yeats just shrugged.

We stood listening to this sweet little brown bird of the

forest and waited long enough so that we wouldn't have to see that man again on the path.

THE NEXT DAY, WE took the 7 a.m. ferry back to the mainland and stopped at a Tim Hortons in Leamington for a coffee and muffin, and chocolate-chip cookies for Yeats. I was feeling lighter after our short trip. Driving the car through the small country towns and past newly planted fields felt like freedom to me.

"I'm looking forward to BC now, Yeats," I said. The trip was less than two months away.

"Me, too," he said from the back seat, where he'd spread out all his books and cookies. "We're going to do some bird-watching, right?"

"I've sent an email to George, to book that Paddle with the Eagles trip he has. Maybe we can do something else in Tofino. Maybe we'll walk the seawall in Vancouver and see some new birds. I don't know what there is in Victoria, but there must be something."

"George again?" he asked.

"Yeah, he's a good guide, and that trip sounds fantastic." Never mind how he'd ignored me that first time around.

"Okay. Have you booked the university tours?" he asked.

"Yes, UBC and UVic."

I'd graduated from Simon Fraser University more than twenty years before, and I thought Yeats might like to see it there on top of Burnaby Mountain, where it was rainy and foggy most of the winter. His favourite weather. But with the university's tour schedules, we could fit in only two of them and decided on the University of British Columbia and the University of Victoria. I was happy he was contemplating university at all.

NINE

LATER THAT SPRING, MY sister Laurie announced that she and her family were moving to Toronto. She came to town to look for a house and I went with her to see a few. It was fun having her around, staying with us in Danielle's room. It reminded me of all those times I'd stayed with her family in London and Greenwich.

I felt welcome and safe in their homes, in a way I'd never felt anywhere else, except at this house I shared with Ben. Whenever I went to visit Laurie and Andy, it felt like coming home, and I'd lie in the guest-room bed immersed in that feeling of belonging.

Years ago, I stayed with them for six weeks in their four-storey walk-up in Chelsea in London. I was recovering from that bout of malaria that I'd picked up on my ill-fated trip to central Africa, and they told me I could stay as long as I needed to. It was just the three of us, before the kids or Ben, and surely the depth of security I always felt in their homes stemmed from that time.

I remember lying on the couch in their living room, under a skylight, reading *The Mists of Avalon*, a big, thick British paperback edition. Every so often I gazed up at the skylight, and once I looked up just in time to see the Concord fly over. I remember walking along the river or over to a place called Neal's Yard, where I sat watching people go by. Bit by bit I recovered my strength and went farther afield, exploring the city. I needed a refuge. Laurie and Andy provided it.

They ended up buying an old house on a ravine in Toronto and planned to move in by the start of the school year. But the house had been gutted and needed to be internally reconstructed. So Laurie continued to come regularly to Toronto to check in on the project and make millions of decisions. I was ecstatic. I had my sister in my house! We rose early and had coffee at the kitchen table. Ben and I took her to dinner to meet some of our friends. I went with her to choose tiles for the bathroom floor and we had lunch with her designer, Christine, who was hilarious.

One morning at breakfast I said to Laurie, "How are the kids with this move?" Thomas was fourteen and Lauren was nine.

"Thomas seems fine. He's very social, as you know, and looking forward to meeting new people. He can't wait to ride the subway on his own, and go downtown with all the friends he's going to make. Greenwich is pretty small."

"How about Lauren?"

"She's upset. She's so shy. She doesn't want to leave her friends in Greenwich. She's really angry, so I promised her a new kitten."

"Jumper will love that," I said skeptically. "What about you? I'm so happy you're moving here that I haven't even asked you! Some sister."

"That's okay." Laurie laughed but looked tired. "It's a lot of work and I'm conflicted about moving back to Toronto. I haven't lived here in more than twenty years. I don't relish the thought of running into old high school acquaintances everywhere I go."

"Don't worry. It won't be like that. We'll take care of you," I said. "I wonder if Yeats and Thomas will spend any time together? Their circles will be completely different."

Laurie shrugged. Thomas was already enrolled in private school, while Yeats was still at Jarvis Collegiate.

"Yeah," she said, "and Thomas is so into sports. Who knows? I'd like to think they'd keep their cousinly friendship going, but dynamics change. Besides, maybe they don't need to see one another all the time to stay emotionally close. Yeats has only one year left at high school, then what? Will he go to university?"

I sighed. "I guess so. He says so. We're going out West to see those schools, but I bet he stays here in Toronto."

"One day, Lynn, you'll have to kick that boy out of the house. He isn't exactly champing at the bit to go, is he?"

Later that day, Yeats came home from school and said, "I hate school. It's useless. They don't teach us anything and there's no point. Really — what's the point? It's not like I'm going to do anything anyway. I'm not going to be a doctor or a lawyer or a banker or anything. I'm not going to be an engineer. So what's the point?"

I couldn't believe I had to go through this all over again, but it was spring and exams were coming up and essays were due, so he was feeling more pressure. This time, I tried a different tack. "What about your friends? What do your friends say?"

"Say about what? I can't tell them how I really feel. They're all so into it. They want to be psychologists and brain researchers and stuff like that. They wouldn't understand."

"Well, is there an assignment that's bugging you right now? Something you haven't started that's due?"

"There are assignments, but that's not what this is about, if that's what you mean." He glared at me. "I just can't see the point of school. It's such a waste of time."

"What would you rather be doing? You could take a year off and do something else."

"Sure I could. That's illegal. I have to stay in school. I have to finish high school and then I have to go to university and make something of myself and be just like everyone else."

I resisted the urge to sing that Pete Seeger song about little boxes made of ticky-tacky. Instead I said, "You do have to finish high school. You're right about that. But you know that you don't have to go to university. You certainly don't have to be like everyone else."

He snorted. "Right."

"And you don't have to decide in Grade 11 what you're going to do for a career."

"That's what you think."

"Look at Rupert. He quit university after a month and has worked all this time. University wasn't right for him, right out of high school, but he'll go back. I think he's gearing up to go back, actually. There are options. You could travel or volunteer or work." I felt like a broken record.

"Maybe. But do you really think Rupert is happy working in the store?"

"I don't know. Is this about happiness, then?"

"Of *course* it's about happiness. What's the point otherwise?" He turned away and mumbled, "Maybe I'll end up on the streets."

This comment alarmed me because it was new. I felt like breaking down as I watched him disappear upstairs and heard his door slam. I felt like flinging myself to the floor and screaming because I couldn't make everything perfectly okay for my boy. I just couldn't do that. And I knew that, in a way, he was right. If a person didn't have a clear sense of direction, how did they find their path? It was a big, scary world out there, full of responsibilities and choices—would he be ready?

The conversation exhausted me. We had a version of it weekly, which, I suppose, nicely balanced all my otherwise good cheer.

When Ben came home that night I told him what Yeats had said.

He said, "I can't believe you engage with him when he's like that."

"What am I supposed to do? Walk away? Tell him his feelings are wrong?"

Ben shook his head and stared at me. His mother had had three teenaged sons to deal with and I had a feeling she'd done it mostly at arm's length. Or maybe her boys hadn't brought their angst home the way Yeats did.

"I can't imagine just ignoring him when he needs someone to listen," I said.

"Yeah, but look how much it upsets you. You get all tied up in knots. It isn't worth it."

"Yes, it is." *Isn't it?* I was in the habit of listening to Yeats; I had been ever since he was small, when we spent so much time together. I'd engaged in all his activities, learning from him as he learned from me. *But maybe it's time to let go a bit more*, I thought, thinking of that stuffed-animal dream.

While Ben and I were talking, Yeats was up in his room listening to Jesse Winchester. He was fine. He just needed to vent and I was the safest person to do it with, exactly as his mentor had said. My friends with older children told me that if I was able to keep the lines of communication open with Yeats, even when what he had to say was ugly, then I should count myself lucky.

And this was what happened nearly every night: I brushed my teeth, changed into my pyjamas, and fluffed up my pillows in anticipation of a good read. Then I climbed into bed, made sure my alarm was set, and opened my book.

Somehow, no matter what time this ritual took place, as soon as I'd read two pages at most, Yeats came crashing into the room and flung himself across the foot of the bed. He demanded, simply by his presence, nothing less than my complete attention.

And always, I put down the book with an inward sigh and looked at my son. He was ready to talk, sometimes to vent anger or frustration, but always to talk. How could I possibly send him away?

Even on those evenings when I was dead tired and wanted only five minutes to read before conking out, I couldn't ask him to leave. What if he decided to go to university in BC, or even in Guelph? No. I gave him my attention, listened to his stories, tried to calm his fears. I thought of those friends who considered me lucky that Yeats still talked to me, and if he was particularly upset about something, I clung to that thought. He felt safe with me because I'd been an emotional haven for him all these years, and now that he was a teenager, I couldn't just send him away. These sessions seldom lasted very long, and I had a feeling that one day they'd stop altogether, and I knew I'd miss them. So I always, no matter when, listened patiently while he expressed himself.

I TURNED FIFTY THAT June. I decided against a big party and had two dinners out instead. The first was with Mom and several old friends. It was a low-key party, but some friends brought me flowers and others gave me small gifts. I felt loved by these special people.

The next night was dinner with all our four children and Greg's family. It was considerably more raucous with the two little boys along, Taylor and Noah, and I felt blessed to be their beloved auntie and to be surrounded by the love of these people, too. Rupert and Danielle wrote me heartfelt messages about how special I was to their lives, which made me shed a few tears. How could I not? I'd always found solace in family life and although we didn't express our love for one another all the time, I felt their affection deeply.

Turning fifty coincided with Yeats finishing Grade 11. He had only one more year of high school. Before I knew it, it was time for our BC trip. Yeats assured me he was looking forward to visiting UBC and UVic, to reconnecting with my friends up and down Vancouver Island, and to taking more bird tours with George the Birdwatcher.

Fear came up again, though. I didn't have my usual pre-trip buzz. I felt a reluctance to get ready, an unwillingness to bring up the bags from the basement or to think about what to pack.

I'd already arranged everything: the rental car, the hotels in Victoria and Tofino, the campus tours at the University of British Columbia and the University of Victoria. I'd spoken to the friends who would be hosting us. Everything was ready but me. I didn't want to go. I did want to go. I was dreading it. I was mad that I was dreading it. I dragged the bags upstairs—brand-spanking-new bags that replaced the ones we lost in the shipwreck—and when I opened them up and smelled their plasticky scent, the dread dug in a little bit deeper.

The short trip to Pelee Island had not prepared me for this longer trip after all. Even though I was going with Yeats, I was leaving Ben behind. I could see it in Ben's eyes, too: he didn't want us to go, either.

He said, "Come home to me, baby. Don't forget." I wondered if he was thinking of the shipwreck when he said this, or if he simply understood the pull of the West Coast for me.

I knew everything would be all right and I knew I'd be glad to be there and that, yes, part of me, the part that belonged in BC, wouldn't want to come home. But I would come home.

I said, "How could I forget?"

I resented this new feeling of not wanting to travel. I kept repeating to myself, *I love to travel, I love to travel*, but the darkness at the heart of the fear didn't dissipate.

We were in Vancouver for only two nights, staying with my old piano teacher and friend, Marnie Carter. We loved Marnie for her big heart and active interest in what everyone was doing. At seventy-five Marnie still taught piano, but only to adult students, and she was as busy and fit as any young person I knew and more so than most.

She picked us up at the airport, fed us dinner, and then took us down to Jericho Beach for a stroll along the boardwalk.

"I need to keep you two up tonight until at least 8:30,

so you won't be jet-lagged tomorrow," she said, and she was right.

But I struggled to keep up with her as she strode past volleyball courts full of scantily-clad young people, families eating ice cream cones, zillions of dogs on leashes. It was a gorgeous night and all of Vancouver was outdoors. We decided on a meeting place because Yeats wanted to look for birds while I was trying to stay awake and catch up with Marnie. He was zonked, too, but couldn't pass up an opportunity to see a bird species that wasn't in Ontario.

Once Yeats veered off the path, Marnie said, "Now tell me all about what you're doing. And how is your mother? How is the store? What are your plans in Tofino? Are you going to visit Martha and Dado?"

"I spoke to Martha and we're planning on seeing them, maybe staying a night." Martha, one of Marnie's daughters, had been a friend of mine since Grade 9, the year we'd lived in Vancouver after we took that family trip across the country. "I guess Yeats is about the age now that Martha and I were when we met."

"You girls were inseparable."

"For a year, and then we moved again."

"But you came back and went to Simon Fraser. Maybe Yeats will follow in your footsteps."

"That's part of why we're here, to see about universities. I just want him to stay in school and if he decides to come here, I'm sure he'll love it as much as I did."

"If he moves out here, we'll take care of him!"

Yeats saw four new birds that evening on the beach: bushtits, violet-green swallows, glaucous-winged gulls, and Brandt's cormorants. All four of these birds are found only in the West.

Bushtits are tiny and completely grey. Unlike most birds, bushtit family members all sleep together during nesting season. Vancouver is the northernmost part of their range in North America, and we were fortunate enough to see a large group of them (I was there for that) hanging upside-down in low trees. Eating, perhaps: bushtits forage for insects and spiders while hanging upside down by one foot and using the other to push leaves aside.

The violet-green swallow is similar to our tree swallow in appearance and behaviour, but, like the bushtit, it is found only in the West. These birds are a joy to watch as they swoop and soar, catching insects in flight and gleaming green and blue in the sunshine.

"Glaucous," according to some sources, means "light bluish-green." I think you have to see these glaucous-winged gulls up close to believe their wings aren't just grey, like those of most of our gulls. Or maybe the name just doesn't fit. In French, actually, they're called *goélands à ailes grises* — grey-winged gulls.

Gulls are among the most difficult birds to identify. We own a huge bird guide that is devoted to gulls of the Americas, and I go practically blind flipping the pages and trying to get them straight. I never will. These glaucous-winged gulls are quite large — around 55 centimetres compared with the

45 centimetres of the very common ring-billed gull that most Torontonians are familiar with—and their wingtips are not black or white, but of the same grey as their wings. Most gulls have black or white wingtips. That's just one of the little facts I might never have known before I started reading bird books.

The Brandt's cormorant, too, is found only on the West Coast, from Alaska to southern California, and exclusively in ocean environments, breeding where the California Current brings its favourite foods to the surface. The name "cormorant" comes from the Latin *Corvus Marinus*, meaning "marine crow." Its scientific name, *Phalacrocorax*, is from the Greek for "bald crow." Clearly, whoever named this bird was seriously reminded of crows, perhaps because of their black feathers and habit of perching in high places after a meal. They don't sound like crows, though. The Brandt's cormorant makes almost no sound at all, just a low quacking, audible at only a short distance.

THE NEXT MORNING, YEATS and I took the bus up to UBC and went on our campus tour. It was raining, which was too bad because I wanted Yeats to see the view of the mountains and the harbour from the university. A well-informed undergrad showed a group of us around, pointing out engineering and chemistry buildings and taking us to see a typical residence room. She told us they had regular maid service, something I sure didn't have when I lived in residence! She took us to see Nitobe Memorial Garden, a traditional Japanese garden right on the campus. It was stunning, lush and serene. The tour took us only a few steps inside it, so we could get the general idea. We saw an arched bridge over a pond, stone statues, and pathways winding off into the trees.

I said to Yeats, "Let's come back here once the tour is finished and have a proper look around. Maybe have lunch in the tearoom."

He said, "No. This place is incredible. If I tour it, I want to be alone. Sorry, Mom."

There it was again. I had to accept that there were places he really didn't want to go with me.

I said, "But we may never come back here. Let's just take this opportunity."

"If we never come back, we never come back. This is a place I'd want to be by myself in."

I couldn't change his stubborn old mind.

Not much later, when we were standing beside an outdoor sculpture, Yeats leaned in to me and whispered, "See this tree?" He patted an enormous trunk beside us. I nodded. "It's a cedar. Like those scraggly ones by the beach at the cottage." I laughed out loud and the tour leader looked over at me. Yeats left his hand on the tree and mouthed at me, "Fantastic tree!"

Marnie drove us to the station to catch the bus that would take us to Tsawwassen and the ferry to Victoria. When she dropped us off she said, "You two are welcome back here any time. And Yeats, if you decide to come west to university, I'll take care of you the way I took care of your mother, all those years ago." She laughed.

"'The circles of our lives,'" I said, as Marnie hugged me. "Thank you."

The crossing to Victoria was beautiful: misty and rain-soaked. Yeats stayed out on deck for the duration of the ferry ride, not dancing away as he did that time we went to Nanai-mo, but standing solitary, looking out to sea. He saw his first pigeon guillemot, a black-and-white member of the puffin family. And he got to stand in the freezing-cold rain.

"Mom, it was the best thing ever!" he said to me later.

I, on the other hand, didn't feel my usual joy to be on the ferry. In fact, I wondered if I was capable of feeling that joy at all anymore. After that moment at Fish Point on Pelee Island, that openness had been buried again under anxieties and practicalities, responsibilities and day-to-day life. I wanted to feel carefree, even for a moment. I asked the universe for some carefree.

I rented a car in Victoria and we decided to take the scenic route up to the university from our inn near the harbour. It was a sunny morning and we stopped at oceanside parks along the way to look for birds. Something smelled amazing, heady, as though a million flowers had opened all at once and spilled their scent over everything. We saw lots of birds, but no new species.

I was impressed with the campus at UVic. It was small compared to UBC's, and maybe because of its size, it felt more comfortable to me. There were a lot of trees on campus — even, at one end, a forest — as well as lovely lawns covered in rabbits, something UVIC is apparently famous for. But I was surprised we couldn't see the mountains from the campus. Here we were, in one of the most scenic places in the world, with no surrounding scenery. Everywhere we went I looked for a glimpse of ocean or mountain. Maybe we weren't taken to the right places, but I found this lack of view disappointing.

Yeats said, "It's too far from everything."

"There are loads of buses into town." I gestured at the parking lot, full of city buses. "Or maybe that's not what you mean. Is it too far from home?"

He nodded. "Maybe that's what it is. It's pretty far from home."

We'd come a long way for a short tour of this university, but that's how it was sometimes and I wasn't sorry. We drove back downtown and met my friends Kate and Marc and some of their five children and went on a boat tour of Victoria Harbour. The sun was out, the breeze gentle and smelling of the sea. Back on shore, crowds gathered to watch magicians and acrobats on the quayside.

Kate said, "Are you sure you don't want to move here?" Then she laughed, because she knew I was torn. "If Yeats comes to school here, we'll take care of him, or at least have him for dinner every once in a while."

Take care of him — those words again. I remembered how Marnie used to have me to dinner when I was at SFU and how I sometimes even spent the weekend. Her home was a haven for me, a place where I felt welcomed and loved, and I knew that if Yeats chose to move west, he'd find that kind of refuge with my old friends.

NOW THAT THE CAMPUS tours were done, we headed back to Tofino for some quiet time together in nature. This is where our birding would really begin, and we were looking forward to resuming our West Coast adventure. I had booked two tours with George: a morning walking tour and a day-long Paddle with the Eagles.

George picked us up at 7:30 on our first morning in Tofino, at Middle Beach Lodge, the same place we'd stayed the last time. He didn't remember us. It *had* been two years, and I figured he saw a lot of people passing through, but how many long-haired teenaged boys named Yeats had he met? People usually remembered Yeats. It didn't matter, though, and I knew that if I mentioned it, Yeats would rightly scowl.

We returned to the path along the shore where we'd walked with George before, and this time we saw masses of hummingbirds. At the cottage in Muskoka we often saw ruby-throated hummingbirds, though usually only one, sometimes two, at a time. But here there were dozens of them buzzing around. These were rufous hummingbirds. George told us he'd had an Anna's hummingbird at his feeder lately, but there weren't any here.

The rufous hummingbird is gorgeous but, as with all hummingbirds, it's impossible to see its features unless it rests for a second on a branch. These were moving so quickly, beating their wings fifty to sixty times per second, that all their colours blurred together. Every so often, though, one would perch, and we would have a good look. The males have a throat of scarlet jewels overlaying a white breast, a brownish-red back and tail, and greenish wings. The female is similar but has fewer jewels at her throat.

We saw orange-crowned warblers for the first time, along with a host of other warblers and sparrows. The orange-crowned warbler is a dull grey-green. The male we saw had a fairly bright yellow chest, which was consistent with the subspecies we knew were found in BC, but we couldn't see the tiny slash of dull orange on its crown. We took George's word that it was there and ticked it off our list.

George brought us to a seashore lookout, where we saw common murres, Pacific and red-throated loons, rhinoceros auklets, and black and surf scoters. George took it all in stride, of course, this being his backyard, but for us all these seabirds were magnificent. Most of them were well past the range of our binoculars, so George set up his scope and we took turns looking at them while he talked.

The common murre is a black-and-white duck-like bird, a bit smaller than a mallard. It nests on cliffs and spends most of the winter at sea. Its eggs are so pointed at one end that, if set in motion, they will wobble around in a circle, a useful adaptation for eggs laid on rocky ledges.

The Pacific loon is the most abundant loon in North America. It spends its entire life at sea except for about three months of the year, when it breeds on land. Tofino is a bit far south for this bird, but there was no doubt about what we saw—grey head, black and white stripes on the side of the neck, checkerboard pattern on the wings. It was a beauty.

The red-throated loon is less out of its range in these parts and very distinctive, with its red throat and smaller size. Though this was the first time Yeats and I had seen one, it wasn't the first time we'd *thought* we had. One late fall at the cottage, we were standing at the top of the hill, looking down on the lake. Yeats saw something he didn't recognize and luckily (or typically, I guess) we had our binoculars. We were very excited to think we were looking at a red-throated loon on its migration down from Hudson's Bay, but when we checked the guidebook, we realized it was a common loon in winter plumage.

The rhinoceros auklet is a stocky, puffin-like bird that also spends most of its life at sea. In breeding season, both adults have a vertical white "horn" where the bill joins the face, giving it its name. No one is sure what this horn is for—maybe just decoration? Loads of birds have decoration, after all. Maybe it's not *for* anything. I became momentarily annoyed with my bird book for implying this horn needed a reason for being. I was happy to have a mystery here and there.

The scoters are both black, medium-sized ducks. The black scoter is all-black with an orange bill, while the surf scoter has a white patch on the back of its neck and a multi-coloured bill. They were hard to tell apart through the scope, so again, we took George's word that we were seeing what he said we were seeing.

A couple in their early twenties climbed up to the lookout and joined us. They were wearing cut-off jeans and flip-flops. The woman was wearing a nearly see-through peasant-style top and lots of silver and turquoise jewellery. They both had long blond hair. Before I could stop myself, I'd pigeonholed them as surfing hippie wannabes. Well, I'd been there, too, except for the surfing, so I suppose I was kind of envious. I didn't look like that anymore, though I wasn't exactly corporate, either. I still had long hair (which used to be blonde) and I wore silver and turquoise, too. But I *felt* different. I wondered: even back when I dressed like a hippie, did I feel like one? *Could* I feel like one? Was I ever ready to drop out and turn on, or whatever it was? I don't think so, and certainly the responsibilities of family and house took away any bit of hippie I might have had left. I'd have to remember to ask Ben how he felt about this. He still looked the part of ageing hippie, with his long grey hair and his peace-sign button, but I wondered if he, too, felt like he'd moved on.

The young man looked peeved, like he'd rather be surfing or drinking coffee on the deck. The woman, though, was full of life. She said, "What do you see? Are there any loons or scoters?"

George's eyebrows shot up and he said to me, "Do you mind if we let her look?"

"Of course not," I said, smiling at the woman.

"Groovy, thanks," she said. She actually said "groovy" —

I wondered if she'd picked up the word from her parents or if it was making a comeback.

Yeats stood stony-faced throughout the entire episode and later, when I asked him if he wished he were a hippie in Tofino, he said, "No." Then he gave me a look that said, *Why are you asking?* "I don't belong here. And I'm not a surfer."

I didn't reply, but I looked at him with curiosity and wondered where he did belong. When I was a teenager I belonged with my family but wanted to get away from them, to explore other possibilities. Looking at Yeats, I wasn't sure if he needed to get away at all.

"Where do you belong, Yeats?"

He shrugged and strode ahead of me. George brought up the rear with his scope and tripod, and I tried to remember how confusing life was as a teen.

THE NEXT DAY WE met George in a parking lot down the highway. He was taking us on a canoe trip to see the eagles. He had a large war canoe on a trailer hitched to his truck. Two very nice Australian women who were coming with us to look for eagles were sitting in the back seat. They were not birders, but they were staying at George's B&B and had decided to take advantage of this expedition to see some of wild Canada.

Wild it was. We drove for ages down an unpaved road to Kennedy Lake, the largest inland lake on Vancouver Island. For the entire drive there was nothing to see but forest. George told us that most of it wasn't virgin forest. It had been logged long ago and, if it wasn't for the activism of people like him, it would be up for logging again. The fight against logging in various watersheds has gone on forever in BC. This particular fight had been successful for the conservationists—for now—but there was a feeling, accurate or not, that if they let down their guard, the logging companies would slip right in.

It was an earthshaking experience to be at the side of the road when a logging truck barrelled past. It was a big rig piled high with trees, some of them over twelve metres long. The truck made the earth rumble; it could surely knock over anything in its path. A second truck followed it. And then, more: one truck followed after another, and pretty soon I realized that I'd just watched half a forest rush by. It was overwhelming and confusing, because what was the solution to resource extraction? Some people would say, "What is this problem that needs a solution?" It was a matter of perspective.

The argument over clear-cutting forests becomes visceral, though, when you see the deforested land from the highway or feel those trucks rumble by. A friend of mine who lives in Victoria told me that most of the clear-cutting took place far from the highways of Vancouver Island. The casual observer, even the intrepid traveller, had no idea of the extent of the cutting. It was a political issue as much as an environmental one, to say nothing of aesthetics, and the logging companies tried to keep their work out of sight.

George talked to us about the clear-cutting, and about

all the jobs he'd had, until nearly an hour later we were at a campground, ready to launch our canoe. He discovered that he'd brought along one too few life jackets for the group. We looked at one another. It was way too far a drive to go back.

One of the Australian women said, "Do you think I could wear one? I'm awfully afraid of water."

"Of course," George said. "And you'll get one, too, since you're a guest in our country." He threw life jackets to both women. He said to Yeats, "You'll sit in the bow, so you get a jacket. And I have to wear one since I'll be steering."

Yeats looked at me, since it was now obvious I'd be the one going without. His look was curious, like he was waiting for me to say something, but I was waiting for George.

George said to me, "Are you a strong swimmer?"

"I can swim. I'm not afraid of the water." I looked at the Australians and said, "We spend our summers on a lake, in boats." I didn't say anything about the shipwreck and neither did Yeats. To be honest, it didn't even cross my mind.

"Okay then," George said. "You can sit in the centre of the canoe. You won't be paddling, so you don't need a life jacket anyway." Hmm. He seemed happy with his logic, which seemed to support my theory that George thought I wasn't really there. But life was short and I didn't argue.

The canoe had a tiny engine on it, a 6 h.p., which took us from our little beach on Kennedy Lake around the corner to Kennedy River. The idea was to paddle down the river while we were looking for birds and to use the engine when we needed to get going. I sat up straight in the middle of the long canoe, feeling like a princess. It was nice not to wear a life jacket, even if it was against the law.

The river was mirror-still. We were gliding on glass and all the trees and bushes on either side were reflected perfectly in the water, upside down. It was as though everything had two matching parts. That dead tree over there had an exact replica, branch for branch, twig for twig, still as stone, in the water. From this distance, the riverscape didn't look like scenery. It was more like being in some kind of weird funhouse where your brain can't believe what your eyes are telling it. We marvelled out loud for a while but found we didn't have enough words to describe the wonder of our surroundings and soon fell silent. We each drank it in alone, this incredible stillness.

We motored very slowly down the river for about twenty minutes. The steady vibrations from the engine and the hard metal seat, and probably a spiritual component I can't name, combined to gently shake my spine and shake my spine until finally I felt a little *clunk*. That misalignment in my sacrum had finally been corrected. I felt the relief instantly and wanted to shout for joy, but that might have startled everyone, so I stayed quiet. In fact, it remained corrected for the next eight months, longer than anything any chiropractor had ever been able to do. I was overcome with gratitude — to this river, to this boat, even to George — all of it had facilitated this healing.

We saw a lot of bald eagles on this trip. We saw so many that eventually we became blasé. My friend Heather, who spends summers on De Courcy Island, said that for them, seeing bald eagles was like us seeing ravens at our cottage. No big deal. They saw them every day. Kind of pesky. But when I lifted my binoculars and saw five eagles at once, I was wonderstruck. Three circling overhead and two sitting on branches, imperious, unbeholden. We were in their habitat and they cared nothing for us, or maybe they hated us and our plastic bags and the noise we brought to their river.

We floated and gazed at the eagles and didn't say too much. My mind drifted, let go a bit. I dipped my fingers into the freezing water. I looked around at the stunning scenery. Beautiful British Columbia. Out here on this river we could see hills on one side and, in the distance, the interior mountains of Vancouver Island. Most of the rest of the view was flat: river, reeds, a few trees, low clouds, more river around the bend.

On our way to the picnic spot, the halfway mark in the tour, we saw a few other bird species: song sparrow, common yellowthroat, spotted sandpiper, lesser scaup, mallard, rufous hummingbird. It wasn't a long or impressive list, but the point of this trip was seeing the eagles, so our expectations weren't high for spotting other birds. The Australian women were happy with everything they saw because it was all new to them and this made the rest of us happy, too.

We passed an abandoned First Nations fishing station and continued around a bend in the river to a little island. We tied the boat to an overhanging tree and scrambled out with our packed lunches. It was hot, but there wasn't much shade on these rocks, so we pulled our hats down farther over our brows and ate. No one said very much, not even George, and after about twenty minutes we set out back the way we'd come.

On the way back, Yeats spotted a bird from the bow. He gave a yelp and reached for his binoculars with one hand and his guidebook with the other.

George instantly stopped paddling and said, "What is it? Where is it?"

"In there." Yeats gestured into the foliage in front of us. "It's hopping around, down low. It's some kind of flycatcher."

This really caught George's attention. "Some kind of flycatcher," he mumbled, before reciting the kinds it could be. We all sort of saw the bird. It was elusive. It was shy. It seemed to be playing coy with us, although it was probably just catching its lunch.

Yeats and George saw different things. Yeats was thumbing through his Sibley and George through his Peterson.

George said, "I think it's a great crested. It's got to be. Look at it."

I tried to see it through the foliage, but it was obscured.

"No, it's an ash-throated," Yeats said. "It's too pale for a great crested. I see those all the time in Ontario."

"But I think the wing feathers have a bit of yellow on them. The ash-throated only has yellow on its belly."

"I don't see the yellow on the wings. Its bill is all black. The great crested has a brown bill." They were looking from their books to the bird, while trying to steady the canoe against the shore as the unnamed flycatcher hopped along. The Australian women looked at me and we laughed silently.

"Whatever it is, it's an accidental," George said. "But I won't be calling it in."

"Why not?" Yeats asked, while trying to see the bird through his binoculars. "I'm sure it's an ash-throated. It looks like nothing I've seen and I've never seen an ash-throated."

I said, "I don't see how you can tell from this distance through all that foliage."

I felt Yeats's and George's eyes boring into me.

George said, "I won't call it in because other birders don't believe me when I call in accidentals from Kennedy Lake. I'm the only one who tours in here, so they'd have to come with me, and if they never found it, they'd think I was making the whole thing up."

I was a bit surprised that other birders didn't believe George when he called in accidentals, but I was too polite to press him about it. I didn't understand the first thing about the politics of birding, anyway.

Later, Yeats said to me, "I wanted it to be an ash-throated because I've never seen one before and he wanted it to be a great crested because there's never been a sighting of one on Vancouver Island. People have seen ash-throateds here before. Either way, it's an awesome sighting. Neither of those birds is supposed to come here."

"Maybe it was neither. Maybe it was something else." I was just bugging him.

He shrugged and looked away, annoyed.

As we were motoring our way back to land, I was remembering when Yeats was small, three or four years old, and we were alone on the island in Muskoka. We were inside and out of the corner of my eye I saw something move from the garden into the forest.

"Look, Yeats, what's that? It's huge."

"Where?" Yeats stood on the couch and peered past me. "A turkey! It's a turkey! It's running away!"

I grabbed my camera from the table and snapped a couple of pictures as it ran into the forest. This was in the days before digital photography, so we had to wait until I finished the roll of film to take it in to be developed.

In the meantime, we looked up turkeys in one of our guidebooks.

"Did you know that in the wild, turkeys can grow to be eight kilograms, sometimes even more? That's nearly ten times the size of a sparrow."

"Well," said Yeats, "we get to see how big they are at Thanksgiving when Uncle Greg carves them up. They're huge."

"Right. And did you know that by 1900, wild turkeys were almost completely gone? Wiped out."

"What happened to them?"

"Hunters. First hunters killed them all and because of development, houses and stuff, their habitat was ruined. Then, hunters saved them. The hunters wanted to keep hunting them so they began issuing licences. Only a certain number could be killed every year in certain places. Also, they started conserving their habitat. People started breeding wild turkeys in captivity and reintroducing them to the wild."

"So there are lots now? Still being hunted?"

"Yes. Millions now, up from nearly gone. I guess that's a success story for conservation. An example of how the Endangered Species List can work."

Not long after that little nature lesson, everyone came back to the island and we told them our story.

"We saw a turkey!" Yeats was jumping up and down. "It was running into the forest!" He imitated the turkey and everyone laughed. They didn't believe us.

My brother said, "I've never seen a turkey in Muskoka. Are you sure we get them?"

My sister said, "You guys were seeing things." No one believed us, or maybe they thought we'd seen something other than a turkey.

Whenever the topic came up, which it did quite a bit, Greg started singing the Partridge Family song (somewhat bastardized), "Point me...in the direction of Al the Turkey..." Yeats was indignant and insulted at first but eventually decided to laugh it off. If he'd ever seen *The Partridge Family*, he might have been less forgiving.

When I got the photos back, we could see something disappearing into the trees. To Yeats and me it looked just like a scrawny turkey neck with a turkey-shaped head on top. Although the body was hidden in bushes and trees, it was unmistakable to us. To everyone else it was a total figment of our imagination.

But over the next few summers we started getting turkeys on the island, or at least on Fairylands Island, next to us. We took the canoe into the little bay and heard them deep in the forest, *gobble, gobble, gobble*, like demented ogres from a fairy tale.

And then, one summer, we had a female with six chicks right on our property. She paraded them around the perimeter of our field, and we watched as they ate bugs and scraped the ground with their oversized feet. A week later there were only four chicks, confirming what we all knew about predator and prey.

The next summer we saw a female turkey calling from our island to its chicks over on Fairylands. One by one they flew over, low to the water. The mother *gobbled* and *gobbled* until all her chicks were safely with her.

One night at the dinner table Mom said, "I guess Lynn and Yeats were right all those years ago, when they said they saw a turkey running into the forest."

Everyone nodded and looked at us. Yeats raised his eyebrows at me and shrugged, as if to say, "Too late now." We knew what we'd seen. No one in the family has ever doubted our bird sightings since.

I thought of this episode every time I saw Yeats name a new bird in the field. If he wasn't sure, he'd consult the books. He was methodical and thorough. He'd trained his eye.

So, even though George was the expert here on Kennedy River, I decided to believe Yeats where this flycatcher was concerned. As he said, it was exciting either way. And I'd had an amusing time watching these two passionate people discuss a little bird as it went about its innocuous business in the bushes.

GEORGE CALLED LATER THAT day to see if we wanted to go on a pelagic tour the next morning. He'd be taking a small group of people way out onto the ocean to see seafaring birds, birds that don't come in to shore. We'd see Leach's storm petrels and tufted puffins, as well as pigeon guillemots, marbled murrelets, Cassin's auklets, and maybe even fork-tailed storm petrels. It sounded exciting: four new birds for our list. I consulted with Yeats, my hand over the telephone's receiver.

He shook his head, rolled his eyes, and said, "Two tours with George in one week is enough."

I left it at that. Part of me loved the idea of being out on the ocean, those rolling waves, the smell of salt and all those unworldly birds. Another part of me never wanted to be at sea again.

By the time we left Tofino and crossed the island, Yeats was ready to spend some more time with people his age. He was a great travelling companion, but he needed some time away from his mom. Our last week in BC was spent with friends, but we were both conscious of a yearning to be home.

Yeats said, "This has been a long trip. I get why you love it here, even though it almost never rains." (We'd had hot, dry weather for the past two weeks.) "But I can't wait to get back to the cottage."

On the flight to Toronto I asked Yeats about the universities.

He said, "I liked UVIC okay, and the tour of UBC made me think maybe university isn't that scary after all, but I don't want to go come all the way to BC. It's too far from home. I don't like the idea of being so far away."

"Should we visit some Ontario universities, then?"

Even though he was talking quite willingly about applying for schools now that we'd seen a couple, I was still wary. I didn't want to push and push only to be rebuffed at the last minute.

"We don't need to. If I go to university, I'll go to U of T."

"U of T? Are you sure?"

"Yup. And I'll live at home."

That was what Ben had done. I sighed out loud and Yeats looked at me.

"What?" he said. "What's wrong with that? Don't you want me to go to university?"

"Yes, you know I do. And I'd be happy to have you living at home, too, but don't you think it'd be fun to go away somewhere? Even to Trent? Peterborough isn't very far, and there's loads of great birding around there." I thought it would be good for Yeats to be away from family expectations and obligations, to be freer to explore. Living in residence at university would be a great opportunity for meeting new people, and I didn't want him to flat-out discount the idea. It never seemed to occur to him to ask if he *could* live at home. I guess he just knew we wouldn't kick him out.

He didn't reply and I decided to stop bugging him for the time being.

Ben was at the airport to pick us up and enveloped me in a long hug in the arrivals hall.

"Thanks for coming back, Lynn," he whispered into my ear. "I missed you. When you go out West, I never know if you'll come back again."

I sighed. "You nut," I said. "Of course I'll always come back."

Yeats was grinning at us, pleased to be home.

That summer we had West Coast weather—*real* West Coast weather—at the cottage: cold and wet. Yeats said, "This is more like it. This is proper weather."

Every once in a while we'd have a sunny day. I went down to the dock early one clear morning and the sky nearly took my breath away. Its long streaks of pink clouds and tiny slice of new moon filled me with awe and lightened my heart. As much as the West Coast pulled at me, this lake and these rocks, this particular Muskoka sky in the morning, was my elixir.

TEN

IT WAS WINTER AND my heart felt heavy. Each morning when I woke up I had a drop in spirits, wondering if anyone would notice if I stayed in bed all day, if I pulled another blanket up over me and tucked a book into the corner between my arm and all these heavy covers. But of course they'd notice and they would worry as well as protest, so in mid-winter I set aside the heavy-heartedness and hauled myself up.

This was the time of year when the store was most quiet. The fall, with all the launches, events, and readings, and Christmas, with its frenzy of shopping and visiting and family gatherings, had passed. Ben and I had more time to spend together. I helped him to pull returns at the store and he packed up boxes of books to send back to the publishers.

This part of bookselling was like cleaning house: not very exciting, but it had to be done.

Then a day came when I woke to lightness instead. It happened every year, unpredictably, sneaking under the door at night, in through the windows. Was it the lengthening days? Was it the promise of spring? Was it something internal, a switch that flicked because something inside me was sick of the heaviness?

My urge to tuck in dissipated. This spring, 2011, I was more conscious than usual of my renewed cheer. That persistent shadow which had dogged me since the Galapagos trip was fading away.

One morning Yeats said to me, "I need to get out of the city. What about you?"

"We could have a little getaway during March Break, go somewhere for a day."

"Let's go back to Amherst Island. Maybe we'll see some more owls."

THE ROAD THAT LEADS to Owl Woods has never been paved. I wasn't even sure if it was regularly graded, since it was full of potholes and ruts. It was a dirt country road, washboard in places, and in mid-March, parts of it were covered with drifts of thick, sodden snow. We were nearly stuck a couple of times. I had to back up the car, shift into lower gear, and take a run at a little rise in the slushy road, but not too fast for fear of digging deeper ruts into the soft snow.

Yeats said, "No matter what happens, Mom, it won't be worse than last year."

I thought, *We didn't have any trouble on Amherst last year*, but I was concentrating on getting the car unstuck, so all I said was, "What?"

He said, "The shipwreck. It can't get worse than that."

I laughed and drove over the hump of snow onto a drier bit of road. I relaxed my hands and shoulders. *We did not get stuck on the dirt road in the middle of nowhere with no one around and no cell phone.* Next time I would remember to put a shovel in the trunk.

One other car was parked at the trailhead and we met its occupant coming back from the woods. The man was about my age, and he was wearing sensible winter attire and carrying a camera with a two-foot lens.

He said, "Good luck in those woods," and pointed with his camera. "It's dead today. Nothing but dead."

I said, "Dead owls?"

Yeats snorted and the man said, "No. No owls. Nothing. Dead." He gave me a weird look.

I said, "Right."

"There was a barred owl this morning. Only one. I got him pretty good," he said, briefly holding up the camera. "But there's nothing now. Only these." He waved his hand around his head.

"Chickadees," I said, and he nodded.

"They're stalking me. I need owls. I need the boreal owl. In Algonquin last winter I got the snowy and great grey.

Also the long-eared. At home we get the northern hawk owl and the barred. I have lots of photos of them, feeding, flying, everything."

He continued listing his lifetime owl sightings and after a while I thought I should participate so I said, "In Muskoka we get the eastern screech."

"Hmph." He practically rolled his eyes and Yeats laughed. I guess the eastern screech owl wasn't very exciting to real birders. I wasn't very good at this game but I tried again.

"We came here last year and saw three long-eared owls and a snowy."

This time the man nodded in appreciation and Yeats started pawing the crusty snow, impatient to get moving. I didn't understand the etiquette of the birder in the field. How long were we meant to chitchat with this guy?

After another minute we went our separate ways. Yeats and I stepped out of the bush into a meadow and immediately two white-tailed deer came bounding from nowhere, crossed the meadow, and disappeared into the trees on the other side. If we'd come two seconds later, we would have missed them. We stood for a moment and breathed. Yeats spied a hawk circling in the sky and took a look through his binoculars.

"Northern harrier."

Just as we started across the field, the man tramped up behind us. He said, "Maybe three of us will have better luck than one."

I said, "All right," although I knew how much Yeats disliked birdwatching with other people.

The man talked the whole way to the forest, crunch-crunching in the snow. I thought, *Maybe he knows what he's doing—maybe he'll flush out an owl with all his noise.* But I saw how stiffly Yeats held himself and I imagined his upset, his disappointment in being joined by this chatterbox of a man.

Once we were in the woods, we split up to look around; the man was still talking, though with less enthusiasm. I responded to barely a thing he said and Yeats not at all.

Yeats took out a handful of birdseed and held it up for the chickadees. The man came closer to watch, smiling a little, but after a very short time, he turned around and left, heading back towards the cars.

I said to Yeats, "He didn't even say goodbye."

"We weren't very friendly to him, Mom. I wouldn't have said goodbye either."

"Huh." I felt bad then. Would it have been better to tell the guy right away that we didn't want company, or should we have pretended to enjoy having him with us? I carried some guilt over this around with me for a while, staying even more quiet than usual.

We didn't see any owls so we hiked back out of the forest. I thought about Peter Matthiessen's long trek to see snow leopards in Nepal. It was time to re-read *The Snow Leopard*, my most-read book, my favourite work of non-fiction. Then I chuckled to myself—how could I possibly compare these two journeys, his lasting months under difficult and some-times life-threatening conditions, and mine a simple walk in the woods?

For me, the climax of *The Snow Leopard* comes when Matthiessen, a Zen acolyte, finally talks with the abbot of Shey Monastery. The abbot is living in a mountain cave and the men meet on a ledge on a sunny afternoon. The abbot is only fifty-two years old, but walks painfully on twisted, arthritic legs, and it's clear he'll spend the rest of his life on this mountainside, a dubious refuge in Matthiessen's mind. The abbot laughs out loud when Jang-bu, the translator, asks how he feels about this forced isolation. He says, "Of course I am happy here! It's wonderful! *Especially* when I have no choice!"

Every time I read these words I'm deeply moved. They stop me. I sit still and question every bit of my own life and wonder at my small irritations as well as the bigger problems I feel beset by. The way I feel about everything, I realize, is my choice. I reconfirm that, at bottom, where it counts, I am happy, and vow to let that happiness come to the top, too, where it also counts. Making the vow is the easy part.

YEATS HAD A LOT due at school. The university applications had gone in mid-January, two months ago, and this next set of marks would be sent in, too. His usual pattern when under this kind of pressure was to have a nervous breakdown, endure a lecture from me about how capable he was of doing the work, and then finish the assignments.

He spent Saturday writing an English essay without the usual fuss.

On Sunday, however, just after lunch, he called me into his room and started in on a breakdown.

"I have too much to do. I can't do it all. I can't do it, Mom."

"What do you have?"

"A history essay due tomorrow. I've started it but it isn't done. I have to have an outline for my Lit presentation done, too, and all the research for another history project. And I have to come up with a social problem to paint in art. And I have a history test at the end of the week."

I could feel his rising panic and there was always a point in this process when I felt it, too — when I somehow forgot that it wasn't my work, my classes, my expectant teachers, and I let the fearful emotions carry me away. Then I pulled back and breathed and started to talk calmly to him.

"Well," I said, "when is the outline due? And the research? Didn't we already talk about that art project? Aren't you going to do kids not spending enough time in nature or something like that?"

This time, though, he didn't want my help. He didn't want me to comfort him and tell him what a good student he was or give him any of my usual lines. He didn't need help organizing his time, either. I kept on, though, even though I saw I was making no headway.

He covered his face in his hands. I tried not to get frustrated. I felt the anger well up and I tamped it down. What did he need from me?

I felt like walking out of the room, but as soon as the thought crossed my mind, Yeats said, "Don't leave yet, Mom."

So now he's reading my mind, or at least my body language, I thought.

I sat down across from him and said, "You do want to get into university, don't you?" and immediately kicked myself for being so leading, so full of expectation for him.

He said, "I guess so." He dropped his head and mumbled, "But it won't be the end of the world if I don't." Then he looked up at me and said, "I'm not going to fail any of these courses. You don't have to worry. I'll be going to university." He was glaring at me.

"What's the problem, then? I don't understand."

He said, "Mom, what I really need from you, right now, is to hear you say it's okay if I don't get all this work done *on time*."

I stared at him. He repeated what he said, and I thought of my father and my grandparents and all the values we were raised with and how horrified any of them would be to be put into this situation. I heard them all shouting, "It isn't okay!"

"That's all I need," he said to me, knowing full well how hard it was for me to say it.

I put my hand on his shoulder. I found myself laughing and crying at the same time. Then I took a deep breath and said, "It's okay, Yeats." I took another breath and he turned to look me in the eye. There was no escape. I said, "It's okay, Yeats, *with me*, if you hand those projects in late." I was not kidding.

I couldn't believe how hard it was to say those words. We were both laughing and crying now and I was sweating like a pig. I felt like I'd unburdened myself of generations of heavy expectation.

Yeats stood up and said, "Okay, Mom. Now I can do my work."

That night at dinner he said, "It's amazing how much work I'm getting done."

I just smiled. I didn't trust myself to say the right thing and I was happy he could finally work on all these assignments with some peace of mind.

A couple of days later I was out with two girlfriends who have children Yeats's age. I recounted what had happened and one of them said, "I could never have said what you did. Not in a million years. I couldn't even have said that with my fingers crossed behind my back."

I couldn't tell if she was judging me poorly or wishing she could change her mindset, as I had done in that moment with Yeats. I decided I didn't want to know.

WHILE YEATS AND RUPERT — I'd been right about his wanting to go back to school — were working on their university applications, Titus decided he wanted to go back, too. He applied to Seneca College for their digital arts program, and was accepted at their York campus. All four children were going to be in university. Ben and I were happy for Titus. He'd been working in the bookstore for about a year, and was quite obviously miserable. He was a talented artist and needed to be using his creativity for more than making interesting book displays.

I was thinking that when Rupert and Titus both left the store, Ben would have only one full-time staff member other than himself—Simone.

I said to him, "You need to hire someone else. It won't be fair to Simone. She can't do everything. and what about when we go on holidays?"

He wasn't really listening to me. I could hear him thinking, *What holidays?* He'd be saving a lot of money with the two boys off the payroll, but I was worried about the cost of this economy, that he'd be the one to pick up the slack. He'd wear himself to the bone to save some money—and was that really the point of having his own bookshop? Again, though, I had to remind myself that I wasn't the boss, and I knew nagging him would have no effect. But I was worried about him, so when Yeats and I decided to go birding in Burlington, at the Arboretum, I said to Ben, "We're mounting an expedition. Do you want to come?" It was Easter weekend, so the bookstore would be closed.

He surprised me by saying yes, he wanted to spend the day in the forest with us, outside, away from his usual life. I was happy, knowing how hard he'd been working and that some time in nature would do him good. I guess he knew that, too. The shop might be an oasis on Bay Street, but it was right downtown, among towers of concrete and glass.

The Arboretum was part of the Royal Botanical Gardens and included a forest sanctuary called Cootes Paradise. It was full of walking trails and went down to an arm of Hamilton Harbour that, since 1985, had been subject to one of the largest wetland rehabilitation projects in North America. Yeats and I had been there before. We'd seen a lot of birds there and loved the place—a park big enough to feel like a real forest.

We walked from the parking circle through the lilac dell (its over 600 species of lilac not yet in flower, of course) and down a grassy slope to the forest.

I said, "What's that sound?" It was like a thousand tiny buzzers.

We all craned our necks to see up to the tops of the tall maples. Yeats said, "It's waxwings. Cedar waxwings."

Ben said, "There are billions of them. We used to see this in the city." Meaning Toronto.

"You still can, down at Ashbridges, near dusk," Yeats said. "They come in huge flocks to the trees down there."

We walked down to Cootes Paradise Marsh and onto the boardwalk. We were in time to see a red-bellied woodpecker crawl up a dead tree and into a hole. We waited there for a while to see if it would come out again. We stood in the spring sunshine in companionable quiet, just breathing and being. Ben was just as good at this waiting around as Yeats and I were, just as good as he'd been at it all those years before when he took me birding at Riverdale Farm.

Ben fell only once in the forest. He slipped when we saw a deer, a big white-tailed deer that spotted us first and bounded off through the trees. He didn't have appropriate hiking shoes, having never replaced his running shoes after the shipwreck, and with all the rain we'd had the trails were muddy. Ben wiped the mud from his hands onto his jeans and we stood still as stone. The deer doubled back until it was twenty metres away, in a clearing. It nibbled at the grass but was too jumpy to eat.

We saw thirty-four bird species that day. So many birds! The deciduous trees were still bare, so it was easier to make sightings. We saw our first warbler of the season, a yellow-rumped. We saw three barn swallows frolicking in the air, dipping and dancing, and two bald eagles riding the thermals way up high.

We saw a small flock of Caspian terns from a viewing platform in the marsh. A binocular-toting father was up on the platform with his young son, who was maybe nine years old and had binoculars too. The father said to Yeats, "Do you know what those are?" pointing at the terns which were now standing on the muddy bank facing into the wind.

"They're Caspian terns," Yeats said, and the boy looked up at him. "They're our biggest tern, but they're rare in Ontario. Usually you'd see the common tern or, more likely, gulls. The gulls are taking over the terns' habitat."

The boy nodded. He'd probably learned about habitat problems in school.

"See," said Yeats, "here come some gulls, probably ring-billed."

The gulls landed on the mud not far from the terns, who shifted together. The father said to Yeats, "You know a lot about birds."

"He's a birdwatcher," Ben said, with more merriment in his voice than I'd heard in a while.

Later, I saw my first ever wood ducks. We were walking carefully down a steep, muddy path. Between the marsh and us was a wooded area but because the trees were leafless, we could see through to the shore.

Yeats said, "Mom! Wood ducks! Look through your binoculars."

He knew I'd never seen them before and they were beauties. There were two pairs. The females were quite plain, like female mallards, except wood ducks are grey and have a white eye patch. The males, however, were spectacular. They looked painted, with red eyes, burgundy neck and breast, and clearly delineated facial patches of green, purple, and white — everything shining iridescent in the sun.

On our way back to the car we stopped and fed chickadees from our hands, something that, I hope, will never fail to give me a small shiver of delight.

"Maybe next time," I said to Ben and Yeats, "you guys will wear sunscreen." Their faces were beet red.

"No way," Ben said. "Sunburn in April is a dream come true."

Yeats laughed and took one last look through his binoculars at the eagles soaring in the sky.

ELEVEN

IT WAS MID-MAY, AND Yeats's final high school exams were in a month, but we'd promised one another we'd spend the weekend of the annual spring migration at Point Pelee. It seemed cruel to us that the best time for birding happened at such a busy time of year. Exams were looming, but Yeats also had essays and projects due. It may have seemed reckless to make a conscious decision to step outside these responsibilities and take a long weekend to bird-watch. But Yeats was doing well at school and it was spring — we longed to be outside for days on end. And the little taste of Point Pelee we'd had the previous year, before going over to Pelee Island, had made us eager.

Point Pelee is a triangular spit of land that juts seven kilometres out into Lake Erie. It's the farthest south you can go on the Canadian mainland (Pelee Island is farther south, close to the U.S. border), and it's famous as a stopping-off point for birds during their spring migration. Thousands upon thousands of birds fly over the Great Lakes every spring on their trip north to breed, and many of them stop at Point Pelee for a rest and something to eat.

The area was settled in the 1830s and used extensively for fishing, hunting, and logging as well as farming, before it became a national park in 1918. This new status didn't immediately affect much of the earlier activity, and it wasn't until 1989 that duck hunting, the last holdout, was officially banned in the park.

A road goes down the centre of the park, with parking lots and observation areas scattered along the way. There's a good information centre with beautiful forest walks partway down the point. There's also the DeLaurier Homestead area with old farm buildings and more trails. The DeLauriers were among the first Europeans to farm at Pelee and their old farm is now a national museum. On the west side of the point are sand dunes and the crashing waves of Lake Erie. The only people allowed to drive past the interpretation centre and to the tip of the point are park workers. Shuttle buses take birders to the tip, and during migration the very keen will leave at 6 a.m.

In January, I'd spoken to a birdwatcher who'd warned me that the place would be crawling with competitive and sneaky birders. "They hide in the bushes, they don't tell you where they've seen stuff, they aren't nice. They look at you suspiciously, as though you've stolen all the good birds."

This sounded dreadful, not the sort of birding we wanted to do at all, but I didn't really believe him. In all the experiences we'd go on to have at Pelee, nothing would come close to what he described, and I had to wonder if he carried around his disgruntlement wherever he went.

This same birdwatcher told me to book well in advance if we wanted to stay close to the park, and in that he was right. I had started calling places in February and most were already booked for migration weekend. I finally found us a room at a motel just down the road from the park—I guess the fact that it was still available should have been a clue to its condition. I would never stay there again, even though it was only a five-minute drive to the park entrance.

The motel was built around an indoor courtyard that housed the swimming pool and party area. We had sliding glass doors that opened onto a balcony, but as soon as we stepped out we were overcome by the smell of chlorine and the sound of shouting children. The only other window was high up in the door, but it was boarded over, so if we wanted fresh air in the room at night, we were out of luck. The carpet was so grimy underfoot that I didn't want to take off my shoes in the room, something I hadn't experienced since backpacking in Asia on a shoestring budget in the 1980s. At least the bathroom and sheets seemed clean and the mini fridge was working.

We stopped at Wheatley Provincial Park on our way to Point Pelee and saw about twenty species; we saw another ten or so from the car. We added nearly forty species to the list in the three hours we spent at Point Pelee that first after-noon. Altogether, we saw sixty-eight species in one day! It was incredible. This was the most birds I'd ever seen and it left me feeling lightheaded, as though I'd won the lottery.

We didn't have to do much work for most of these sightings. The birds were just there, in the trees or swooping through the air over the marsh. All we had to do was stand still and pay attention and then look closely to make the identification.

For some birds we didn't have to look too closely. In Wheatley, for instance, we saw a red-headed woodpecker for the very first time. It was pecking at a dead tree and climb-ing into a hole. Then it climbed back out and flew over to the next tree. We ended up following slowly along as it made its way through the park, and since there were no other people around, we had it to ourselves.

The bird was unmistakable, with its bright red head, black wings, and white breast. It looked like someone had pulled a red cap down over its head, and the line between head and body was so clean. It was a medium-sized woodpecker, a little smaller than a robin, although the woodpecker's wingspan is considerably larger.

The red-headed woodpecker has some unsavoury habits. It routinely attacks other birds to keep them out of its ter-ritory and will tip eggs from nests, destroy nests, and even poke holes in duck eggs if the opportunity arises. It eats just about anything and will capture grasshoppers and stuff them live into tight little corners, where they can't get away but are stored for later.

I didn't know any of this when I first saw the bird, but it wouldn't have mattered. I could never bring myself to assign moral values to the bird world. All I could do was admire them for their beauty and their spectacular variety.

That afternoon at Pelee we saw the black tern for the first time. Yeats hadn't told me we might see this particular bird, probably because he knew how much I loved terns. He wanted me to be surprised. I'd seen them in books, but I never imagined how beautiful they would be in real life. I stood on the boardwalk beside my grinning son, alternating between holding my breath and gasping in delight.

There were two pairs of black terns and we watched them fly gracefully, swooping around the marshy area, catching bugs. Although the breeding adults weren't completely black—their wings were silvery-grey—they appeared all black in the sky. They were the inverse of all those snowy-white seabirds we were used to. If I was in love with white terns, these black ones turned me inside out.

I nearly said to Yeats that I'd seen enough, now. We could go home.

We continued slowly along the boardwalk, listening to the shushing of the reeds in the wind mixing with the high-pitched "pipping" of the terns. We'd noticed that the terns stopped every so often and rested on one particular part of the railing. We stopped before we reached them and waited. Within a couple of minutes, two terns came to perch. We were three metres away from them, at eye level. I could see the wind ruffling their wing feathers, and watched as they raised and lowered their feet. We took a step or two and they retreated along the railing, always keeping the same distance between us. We stopped and they stopped. No one else was nearby. It was just us and the wind and these gorgeous, joy-inducing terns.

The black tern migrates every year from the north coast of South America. Pelee is just about the southernmost part of its nesting range, so possibly, these birds we saw were headed much farther north. They nest on open water, something I find hard to imagine, and sometimes migrate in huge colonies of up to tens of thousands of individuals.

Eventually we left the boardwalk behind and drove to a place on the west side of the point, with access to the dunes. We were two minutes from the parking lot when a group of people stopped us and one said in a stage whisper, "common night-hawk ahead. There's a woman with a scope who'll let you see." These people were smiling like they'd just caught a big fish.

We proceeded quietly, as we always did, and found the woman with her scope around the next bend. She was tiny, about the size of her tripod, and dressed like a birder, but the vibe I was getting from her was more old-hippie than Mountain Equipment Co-op. I liked her right off and she smiled at us, friendly and open. I couldn't help but think of that Toronto birder who'd warned us against Pelee.

She wanted us to see the nighthawk and told us what to look for through the scope. Although the instrument was trained right on the bird, it was so perfectly camouflaged that she worried we still might miss it.

She said, "It's sitting, tucked into those branches and looks just like them, except for a bar of white, which is a wing patch. Also, you can make out a tiny bit of its striped waistcoat."

Yeats looked first and after a couple of seconds he saw it.

This was the first time he'd seen one at rest. He'd seen five or six common nighthawks flying over Alex's house in Nanaimo the summer before. He said they flew like crazy terns and he didn't know what they were at first.

I looked through the scope and saw a funny-looking bird, scrunched and hunkering on its branch, eyes closed. It reminded me of the cat when he didn't want to be picked up, invoking gravity to his cause.

At the lake we saw flocks of birds way out on the water but we would have needed a scope to identify them. We waited in the hope they might come closer, but gave up after a while and headed back to the motel.

We ate a boring meal in our horrible room, but Yeats was keen to record all these birds. When we first started bird-watching, Yeats took his piece of paper and pencil stub with him, stuffed in a pocket. He stood in the forest after seeing every five species and wrote down the names. After a while, he stopped bringing the list with him. He'd store twenty, thirty, forty species names in his head and write them all down at the end of the walk. Sometimes he'd use the ROM guide to birds as a memory aid; sometimes he'd use me. But usually he remembered them all on his own and listed them in the exact order in which they'd appeared.

He sat on his bed with his books scattered around him and I lay on mine, reading *My Name Is Mina* by David Almond, a book for young teens about a girl who didn't fit in. It was filled with different fonts: sometimes there were only two giant words on one page, for example. I loved that every time I was ready to turn the page, I had no idea what I would find on the other side.

THE NEXT MORNING WE rose at 5:30, ate a quick breakfast, and were in the park by six. We drove behind a long line of cars straight to the information centre. The parking lot was already half full and I thought that we'd finally see the famous crowds of Point Pelee, people hiding in bushes and scowling at one another.

We did see a lot of people milling around waiting for the shuttle to the tip, holding cups of coffee and their long-lens cameras. No one was scowling. In fact, what I sensed from this crowd was excitement and anticipation. These people, like us, were up early to do something they really wanted to do and it was a nice day, overcast but not raining. No one was talking on a cell phone, there were no laptops open anywhere, and no one was hiding in any bushes.

Yeats and I headed off into the forest south of the information centre, having decided to go to the tip later. I was conscious of that moment of stepping into the woods and leaving everything else behind. That one instant when all the sounds of people, of traffic, of doors opening and closing, were suddenly gone, swallowed up by trees and ferns. It was like a curtain falling on a stage, and I waited for that moment every time. My heart opened just a little bit wider. I looked at Yeats and saw it on his face, too. We were alone in the forest now, just us and all those creatures, all those glorious trees.

We saw eastern bluebirds, eastern towhees, great-crested flycatchers, and many different warblers. We kept walking and sighting, mentally ticking birds off every few minutes, hoping to see something new.

The trail through the woods wound around and we wound slowly around with it, occasionally seeing another person ahead, turning the next corner. Around one bend we scared something out of the foliage. We followed very quietly and watched as it settled again, not far away. It was a male bobolink, a new bird for us.

The breeding male bobolink is a distinctive bird. It's the only American songbird that has a white back with black underparts. The back of its head is yellow and it's a bit smaller than a robin. This bird migrates great distances every year, flying south of the equator and back again in the spring, a round trip of about 20,000 kilometres.

This early-morning bobolink was wary of us and hopped back into deeper foliage as we watched it, so we left it to fatten itself up for the rest of its journey north.

Around another bend the trail ran beside a shallow river, which was full of fallen logs and large stepping-stone rocks. I was wandering along happily, my brain unfocused, letting Yeats do the looking.

All of a sudden, Yeats was jumping up and down, just like he used to do as a small, excited child. He was pointing at a little yellow bird that was also hopping, going from log to log in a boggy patch of the river.

Yeats whispered, "Mom! It's a prothonotary warbler! Look at it!"

I gave it a good look because obviously this was a very special bird. Yeats was beside himself with emotion, literally hopping from foot to foot and making little squeaky noises.

Another couple came slowly from the other direction. The woman saw the prothonotary and let out a little shriek. She, too, jumped up and down while her companion looked and nodded thoughtfully. They looked to be in their eighties and I heard her say, "I've never seen the prothonotary warbler, never!" with such excitement I thought she might cry.

I was grinning and the woman's friend was grinning too, but our two birdwatchers could barely contain themselves.

This warbler had blue-grey wings and tail and a black beak and legs, but was otherwise a gorgeous bright yellow. (The name "prothonotary" comes from Roman Catholic clerics who used to wear yellow robes.) They are one of only two species of warbler that nest in cavities, preferably in swampy areas, and in winter they live in mangroves along the north coast of South America. They are listed as endangered in Canada because of habitat erosion, something I didn't know when I was looking at this elusive bird. When I eventually learned about their endangered status and remembered the elation surrounding this sighting, I felt a stab of grief.

We watched the bird for ages, side by side with this other couple, and then continued down the path. Not too much farther along, we saw five or six men who had set up their tripods on a bridge over the river. They sat on camp stools with their coffees beside them, waiting for the prothonotary.

I tried to catch the eye of one of these men to tell him the bird they sought was slowly hopping its way towards them, but they all turned away from us and we stepped around them on the bridge. This was highly anti-social behaviour from all of us. I should have stopped and talked to them. They should have engaged in my effort to look at them. Surely they knew we'd seen the bird from all the energy coming off us? I said good morning and they barely mumbled, looking away. Never mind.

We took a break from birding by going into the information centre to look at the notice board. Someone had put the location of the prothonotary as right at that little bridge. That was where it was yesterday and that was where it would be in about fifteen minutes, to be repeatedly photographed by a gaggle of seated men.

Next, we took a trail that led north from the centre and right away we saw a white-eyed vireo. This was our third new bird! No one else was around to see it, but we'd seen it listed on the notice board, so we'd been hoping it would be there.

The white-eyed vireo is a small songbird, a little bigger than a chickadee, and is mostly a dull mix of yellow, white, grey, and green. It has a bright white iris with a black eye ring. All other vireos have dark eyes.

Not much later we saw our first northern parula, another kind of warbler. Since it was perched up high, we saw its white belly and yellow throat and breast with a necklace of black feathers splitting the yellow in two. It was beautiful.

The parula nests in hanging moss, using Spanish moss in the southern part of its range and beard moss in the North. Not much more is known about its breeding habits, since it does a very good job of obscuring its nests.

When I saw a new bird, one I'd only ever seen in the books before, I always felt a little thrill. It started in my belly and moved up through my chest and into my heart. Sometimes I didn't pay enough attention to this feeling and really only felt it in my head, experienced it as something I *should* be feeling. But during those times when I was truly aware, I experienced this emotion as joy everywhere in my body.

It was late morning by the time we took the shuttle to the tip, which was windy and crowded. The trees growing out there were less dense and had an unsubstantial feel to them, as though the lake might swallow the whole place up at any moment.

We saw a guided tour partway down the beach. Everyone was clumped together and looking up at something in a tree. The bird flew down onto a log and we saw that it was a red-headed woodpecker, another excellent sighting of this striking bird.

We walked past this happy group and out towards the very tip of mainland Canada. People were posing at the point while others snapped their photos. Waves crashed up on the beach and a few people posed in front of the signs warning of deadly undertows.

Neither Yeats nor I had a crushing need to stand at the very tip, so we watched for a few minutes and then turned around and headed back north.

We went straight back to the shuttle bus and then, once at our car, headed to the Homestead area of the park. It was hot by then and we were hungry, so we ate our picnic lunch and then wandered along a meadow path. No one else was about so we sat down at the side of the path and waited for birds to come. Pretty soon, I lay down and said, "Wake me if anything good comes." The sun was hot, the air smelled of sweet grasses, and I was feeling tired after all our walking.

"What do you mean by 'good'?" Yeats asked.

"You know, something new."

"Or an owl? Or a hawk? Or maybe an indigo bunting?"

"Yeah, something like that. I just want to rest a bit."

He let me lie there while he murmured bird names to himself as he spotted them in the field: yellow warbler, song sparrow, yellow-rumped warbler.

Then he said, "Time to sit up, Mom. There's a new bird!" In fact, there were three new birds in quick succession: male bay-breasted warbler, male black-throated blue warbler, and Swainson's thrush.

The two warblers couldn't have looked more different. The bay-breasted is covered in colours: black face, bay breast with russet throat and under-wings, a russet cap, and yellow patches where ears might be. Its wings are blackish with white tips. The black-throated blue is quite elegant looking with its deep blue feathers, white breast, and a bit of white under its wings. Its throat and face are black. The female of this species looks absolutely nothing like the male and for a long time, ornithologists took them for separate species. She is buffy-yellow underneath and olive grey on top. She was probably somewhere nearby, staying hidden, eating her bugs.

The Swainson's thrush looks a lot like other thrushes, with its lovely spotted chest and light brown back. The only real difference is its white eye ring and a slightly reddish tinge to its face.

By the end of the day we had seen seventy-two different species, six of them brand new ones for our list. Spectacular. Yeats spent a lot of time that evening crouched over his list book, scribbling names and adding things up.

AT 7:30 THE NEXT morning we checked out of our motel, loaded up the car, and drove fifteen minutes to Hillman Marsh, a conservation area very close to Point Pelee. It was pouring rain but never mind; I had rain gear and Yeats loved this weather.

There was only one other car in the parking lot. Three people were walking slowly down the path towards the marsh, decked out in camouflage-coloured rain suits, rubber boots, and wide-brimmed hats. One of them was carrying a scope wrapped in plastic.

I struggled into my rain pants in the front seat of the car

and changed into my other pair of walking shoes, the ones without the air holes on top. I pulled on a peaked cap and covered it with the hood of my sweater and then the hood of my jacket. It would have to do. Yeats was wearing shorts, a hoodie over a T-shirt, and his one pair of running shoes. He really didn't mind; if I bought him a rain jacket, he wouldn't wear it. I'd long given up that fight.

I remembered taking Yeats to BC when he was just nine months old. We'd stayed with my friend Alex and her family in Nanaimo. Alex's four-year-old daughter, Breanna, had taken us on a hike that her daycare often did. It went from the school down to the beach and through a ravine of west coast rainforest.

I'd hoisted Yeats onto my back in a carrier and the four of us had set out in a slight drizzle. A staircase of earthen steps had taken us down into the ravine where we were sheltered from the gentle rain, but by the time we were halfway into the forest, the rain had picked up and we were getting soaked.

Alex said, "Lynn, look at Yeats." She was laughing. I craned my neck around and saw that Yeats had tipped his face up and closed his eyes and was revelling in the rainfall.

I said, "Hey Yeats, you're getting all wet." He opened his eyes and gave me a huge smile and then went back to his particular rapture, laughing as the rain hit his face.

The next day Alex had to work, so Yeats and I went down to the waterfront promenade for a walk. It had begun to rain so I pulled out a plastic cover I'd bought for the stroller but had never used: BC seemed like a very good place to try it out. But as soon as I'd put it in place, Yeats fought it. He kicked at it and punched at it and started to scream.

Huh, I thought. *I've seen a hundred babies placidly sitting behind their plastic rain guards, so what's with this?* I took it off and he settled immediately, sticking his hands and face out from under the stroller hood to get them wet.

I gave that cover away.

Yeats was soaked through by the time we got to Hillman marsh, which took less than five minutes. The rain was pouring in sheets and had created huge mud puddles along the path. The three other people were huddled around their scope and barely looked up as we approached. They looked miserable and after about a minute, they packed up and went back to their vehicle.

Yeats, meanwhile, had spotted a greater yellowlegs out in the marsh and was excitedly telling me to look through my binoculars. This was our first sighting of this species and a good augur for the day. Maybe. It didn't always work out that way, of course. We could see a new bird right off the bat one day and not another new one for two months.

The foot-high greater yellowlegs is a common breeder across most of boreal Canada and southern Alaska, but because it nests in swampy, mosquito-infested muskegs, it is the least studied of all our shorebirds. The one we saw at Hillman was on its spring migration, and we watched as it fed on the frogs and small fish that were swimming around its long yellow legs.

While we were watching the greater yellowlegs we spotted

some Forster's terns and some adult male northern pintails, a few of each. We'd seen the terns before, but we'd never seen the pintail. Another new bird!

The breeding male northern pintail is a gorgeous duck with a chocolate-brown head and a white throat, grey sides with a greenish tinge to its wing feathers, and, of course, a long, pointy tail. It is apparently elegant in flight, but we saw it swimming in the marsh, not too far from the tern.

Yeats kept watching the birds and I consulted the map board, which said that the shorter loop around the marsh took about forty-five minutes while the longer one took a couple of hours. Given the weather, we decided to set off on the forty-five-minute walk.

Three minutes later, patches of grass thinned to tussocks and then to sporadic tufts only along the edges of the path. One edge of the slippery path fell off into the marsh and since I was reluctant to test my balance, I followed Yeats's example and just walked in the mud. Every time I lifted my foot, my shoe brought ten tonnes of earth up with it. I shook the foot to dislodge some mud and placed it down again, squelching as I went. It wasn't long before I gave up and resigned myself to very muddy shoes as well as the workout required in hefting them.

Pretty soon my socks were soaked. I longed for boots. An image of the muddy trenches in the Great War flitted through my mind, but I shook it off as disrespectful. I thought *this* was muddy? The rain pelted down and I longed for a warm room with a fireplace and a book to read. I wished for sunshine.

But then I focused on Yeats walking ahead of me, steady and uncomplaining. He turned around and smiled at me, just a small, sweet smile of encouragement as though he'd read my mind.

I wondered, *When did this happen? When did our roles reverse so that now I am the encouraged rather than the ever-encouraging parent?*

Along this edge of the marsh was what appeared to be a nursery school of Canada geese. There were three adults and forty goslings, small and fluffy yellow, so cute. The young were trying to stay up on the edge to eat from the tufts of grass, but every time we got close, the adults made some secret sign and the youngsters rushed back into the water. They swam a ways, climbed out to eat again, and then repeated the process as we encroached once more.

Finally, they'd had enough and decided to swim back in the direction we'd all come from, and we went on without them.

We walked one whole side of the marsh without seeing any birds, but on the next length we saw a pair of killdeers, a couple of spotted sandpipers, and then one Wilson's phalarope in lovely breeding plumage. The phalarope was another new species for us, so we stood in the pouring rain and watched as it stood in the pouring rain.

Seeing these birds in ones and twos was a sobering experience. I'd always imagined birders standing in fields watching great flocks flying past, or being in a forest as hundreds of birds fed from tree to tree. For example, about the northern pintail, our ROM guide says, "Flocks may number several thousand individuals during migration." Why weren't we getting that picture? Was it naïve of me or had the bird population been decimated to the point of near novelty? Or were these just solitary characters, like the ornery chipmunks we had at the lake? Those chipmunks were so grumpy I couldn't imagine them living together to save their lives.

I wondered—if we'd come to this marshy place two hundred years ago, would we have seen a thousand Wilson's phalaropes? Perhaps it was stories of the now-extinct passenger pigeons that used to "blacken the sky" that caused me to expect to see large flocks, and I pondered this as we stood in the rain, two solitary humans.

Back at the car, I took a T-shirt from the trunk to dry my feet and for Yeats to wipe the condensation off the rear window. The defrost was on the fritz. We were two happy drowned rats. Three new species and a very peaceful walk in the rain.

As I was lacing up my dry shoes, a young couple drove up and parked next to us.

The woman rolled down her window and said, "Did you see anything good? Is it worth all this rain?"

"We saw a Wilson's phalarope and a greater yellowlegs."

"Oh! A yellowlegs?"

"Yes. But it's really muddy..."

But they weren't listening anymore; their faces were shining. They were anticipating getting out there, mud or not.

We drove home along the north shore of Lake Erie and

stopped at a couple of provincial parks along the way. The rain was still pouring and it was extremely windy. We were the only people around. At every stop I pulled on my rain pants and soaking shoes, and we trudged along the lake and through wooded areas, hoping to see something. We never did.

The only interesting stop was at Long Point, which is a sand spit that juts about forty kilometres from the north shore of Lake Erie, roughly 200 kilometres from Point Pelee. There used to be a life-sized diorama of Long Point at the ROM. You walked out along pine boards towards a painted scene that depicted the lake with a marsh in front. You stopped at a railing and looked down on stuffed bird and mammal specimens and out at this beautiful painted scene of a summer's day in paradise. We went to see this exhibit every time we visited the museum, probably thirty times when Yeats was small. Come to think of it, this diorama was around the corner from the bird room — a large exhibit filled with taxidermy birds from all around the world. Yeats and I spent a *lot* of time there, marvelling at the tiny hummingbirds and the giant ostriches, and the birds' multitude of colours and shapes.

Each time we went to the bird room we had to look in every drawer and inspect each bird. Sometimes we went with the other children and Ben, and inevitably someone would say, "Which bird is your favourite?" All of us would look up at the hundreds of birds hanging from the ceiling and in the glass cases. Yeats usually went for the smallest ones — the hummingbirds — maybe because he was the youngest. But the Long Point diorama was by far his favourite part of the ROM, and when the museum was refurbished and they took this diorama out, he said to me, "Poor Taylor and Noah. They'll never get to see that." He was crushed.

Only researchers can go to the tip of Long Point. That area has been declared a bird sanctuary and that's a good thing, but we wanted to see something interesting, so we drove as far as we could, to the southernmost campground. Out there, the roads weren't paved, they were made of sand, so in the downpour they were pretty dodgy. I didn't have much experience driving in sand, but when I treated it like slushy snow, the car responded wonderfully.

We parked in a lot ringed by dunes and I put my rain gear back on. I opened my door and it was nearly ripped off the hinges by the crazy wind. We went up one dune but the rain was driving straight into our faces, blinding us. We turned around, crossed the parking lot, and headed up the other dune. It was too loud to speak. Crashing waves, howling wind. We stood for a second at the top of the dune and then Yeats tugged my arm and ran back down to the car. I took in the scene — the lake looked like a roiling ocean, the sky like a scene from the Old Testament, thick with dark clouds swirling across a sun-spackled sky. It was scary and exciting and not for people. The wind had whipped the lake up into a frenzy of rolling waves that crashed onto the beach and right up to the foot of the dunes. There was no way I was going down there, but seeing this wild side of nature quickened my heart, and I had to stop for a few seconds.

I was afraid that if I ran back down the dune I'd fall, so I pushed slowly against the wind and made it back to the car out of breath but exhilarated. While I'd been up there contemplating the wildness of nature, Yeats had been waiting for me in the safety of the car. We were both soaking wet.

A park warden drove up and shouted over the wind that he was locking the gates to this part of the park. It wasn't safe to be out here. We followed behind his truck and left that place.

Yeats said, "That was scary, Mom. We were crazy to think there'd be birds there. Why did we go out?"

"Because we wanted to see what it was like. That's why."

Silence from the boy. Maybe he was too freaked out to contradict me, or maybe he knew I was right. Sometimes you just had to take a risk, step outside, and find out for yourself.

TWELVE

A SUMMER RAIN HAD passed and I was watching the cottage deck dry. Steam rose from it in waves and suddenly there was a dry patch of deck, light brown and hot now with the afternoon sun. Steam off the deck, steam off the roof, imaginary steam coming from the forest. Drops of water fell off the trees; leftover rain and sunlight turned them to gleaming gems. And on the forest floor, shadows of spiderwebs laced with raindrops.

I walked to the top of the hill where the moss was spongy. It didn't crunch underfoot anymore, but gave gently as I stepped, springing back again, green. The rocks were steaming at the top of the hill and everything smelled of the hot Canadian Shield, mixed with the heat coming off the sumac and a hint of juniper. Some of the junipers were dying. These giant junipers expire in the middle first, so that after a couple of years, there was only a large circular green fringe of plant. The centre was all dried, white bones.

Everything has a lifespan.

The air was still after the rain had passed. The sky was clear, the horizon close enough to touch. From the lookout I could see the mass of black cloud receding, moving south, moving west. It was someone else's rain now.

Down below, on the dock, the children were swimming. I couldn't see them through the trees, but I heard their voices, laughter, and splashing as they practiced cannonballs and backflips. I imagined my sister watching the children, standing up because the chairs were still dripping. She was holding a mug of coffee, face turned towards the sun, breathing in this rain-freshened air.

Sometimes, if I sat still for long enough on top of the hill, the broad-winged hawks flew right overhead. One would fly over, then circle back to take a look at me. Then another would appear, and sometimes even a third. One might fly so close that I'd hear the wind whooshing through its wing feathers, imagining I felt that wind against my raised face. My heart would beat faster and I would dig my fingertips into the yellow lichen that clung to the rocks. Then the bird would be gone, just as suddenly, but the power of that encounter would linger and I stayed a while longer, absentmindedly picking at the lichen and gazing out across the lake.

I felt my heart in my breast and my breath in my belly. I heard the laughter from the dock and felt that joy in me, too.

The rain clouds receded, out over the horizon. It was another summer in Muskoka for me, another summer of our kids working in the bookshop and Ben coming up North when he could. Yeats had been accepted at the University of Toronto and so had Rupert, so they'd be off to school together in September. Titus was going to Seneca College and Danielle was in her final year at Western. It felt like a time to breathe easier, a time to be thankful.

BEN WORKED WEEKS FROM Tuesday through Saturday, and then joined us at the cottage until Monday night. He phoned me most nights from the city and we exchanged news of our days. One day he called from work to tell me that part of the tree in our backyard had fallen in a windstorm.

"A big limb cracked right off the trunk and onto the house. Thankfully, the only damage is a dent in an eaves-trough. The limb landed on the house next door, too, but miraculously nothing was wrecked. We were lucky."

"Did you hear it?"

"No. It must have happened in the middle of the night and I slept right through it. You know me."

"Only a bomb would wake you."

"So what do I do? Who do I call?"

"A tree guy."

"What tree guy?"

"I don't know. Look in the Yellow Pages. Best to get a couple of quotes."

"What?"

"Get a couple of quotes to take down the limb. Go with the best one, or the guy you like the best. Your choice."

I thought to myself, *Well, this is good. Let Ben see what kind of work I have to do around the house sometimes.*

He called the next night to say the limb was gone. He sounded proud of himself for accomplishing this domestic task, and so quickly.

The next night Yeats and I went to pick Ben up at the golf club. He loaded all his stuff into the boat and went to park the car. It was a beautiful night, warm and quiet. Yeats and I sat on the back of the boat, looking at the stars. When I saw Ben coming down the dock, I moved forward to turn on the engine.

Instead, I fell. I tripped over Ben's things and started falling into the windshield. I twisted as I fell so that I wouldn't hit the metal point where the windshield splits, and I landed funny in the gap leading to the bow rider.

I cried out. My right shoulder was searing with pain. I'd never felt anything like it. I writhed and screamed for a few seconds before I came to my senses, and then I pulled myself to my knees and grasped the shoulder hard with my left hand, sliding the shoulder back into its socket.

I was sobbing and gasping, and my guys were saying, "What happened? What is it? Are you okay?"

They were hovering over me and all I could think about was getting back to the cottage, where I'd be safe and sound. So I took a deep breath and said, "I'm okay. Let's go."

I drove the boat back to the island, the shoulder screaming at me every time I moved the accelerator stick. I'll never
understand why I didn't get Ben or Yeats to drive. I guess I
was on automatic pilot.

The pain had been cut in half as soon as I shoved the shoulder back into its socket, but even so, it was bad. It already felt
inflamed. All the way back to the island I chanted to myself,
It's getting better, it's getting better, only partly believing it.

I couldn't carry anything so Ben and Yeats took everything up to the cottage. I iced my shoulder and took Advil
and an arnica pill. I rubbed the shoulder all over with arnica
cream. The next morning, after nearly no sleep at all, I did the
same again and Ben took me to a clinic in the closest town,
Bracebridge, to make sure nothing was broken.

The doctor at the clinic said, "You've had a partial sub-
luxation. But I'd expect some bruising." He was turning me
around and looking at my shoulder from all angles.

I mentioned the arnica and he shrugged. "I want you
to go to the hospital for an X-ray to make sure everything
is okay, no bone chips anywhere. Then you can start with
physiotherapy."

Bracebridge had exactly two physiotherapy clinics.
One was attached to the hospital, and was only for its rehab
patients. The other one was booked until September. I found
a physiotherapist who could take me in Gravenhurst, and
Laurie drove me there twice a week for a couple of weeks.
The physiotherapist gave me tiny little exercises to do, which
caused the muscles to cramp and spasm. I stopped with the

exercise. I iced the shoulder and took Advil. I didn't sleep.

Almost every time he saw me, Ben said, "Sorry, heart." Over and over. "Sorry, sorry, sorry."

"It isn't your fault, Ben," I said. "It's no one's fault. I just tripped."

"But you tripped over my stuff. You were picking me up. I shouldn't have put the stuff in the middle of the boat."

"We always put the stuff in the middle of the boat. Stop with the apologizing."

"Sorry." He took on the guilt and that made me angry. Why did things always have to be someone's fault?

I felt like my body was on full alert at all times. If someone bumped into me, I recoiled. If I moved too quickly and jarred my arm, I was rewarded with instant searing pain. I was told not to wear a sling because I needed to keep the shoulder moving, even if it hurt like heck.

I decided to stay at the cottage until Labour Day because there were people there—Mom, Laurie, Yeats, Ben on weekends—to take care of me. I needed someone to do everything, including washing my hair and doing up my bra. It was hot but it hurt to swim. Sharp pains, throbbing pains, itchiness deep inside the socket, strain and sprain in the deltoid. I could only wade into the water at the beach and stand there, feeling sorry for myself. I'd had my last kayak of the season, my last real swim, my last game of badminton in the field. I felt miserable and exhausted by the pain, as well as useless to my family.

The dislocation of my shoulder led to a long season of lulls. Long days sitting in chairs in the shade. Laurie said, "I guess you'll be reading a lot of books." She laughed because that was what I always did anyway and had done since we were kids. She and Greg would be out there running around and I'd be lying on the deck, reading books. Now I had a good excuse.

This enforced rest period coincided with blackberry season, and that year our canes were loaded with fruit. They grew on a steep slope directly in front of the old cottage. From my bedroom window I looked down on ripening blackberries and then out through the birch and hemlock to the shore of the lake. The lake was easier to hear than to see from my window.

I carried a light cardboard container in my right hand and picked with my left. I picked only from the bushes at the very top of the hill and then took the path that led around the hill and picked at the bottom. I couldn't risk the slope, and another fall.

Blackberry canes are prickly and my left hand was not as adept at picking as my right, so most times I came away covered in scratches. As the container filled, it became too heavy for my right shoulder to hold so I returned to the kitchen, dumped the berries into a bowl, and went back with the empty container.

Picking blackberries was one of the few ways I could contribute to meals. I couldn't chop vegetables or wash or dry the lettuce in the salad spinner. Everything I did was at half my usual pace. But everyone loved the berries on their ice cream or morning cereal.

I found a flip-flop in the blackberry bushes closest to the cottage. I picked it up and put it on the deck and kept an eye out for the other one for the rest of the summer. It belonged to Lauren. The kids had been playing Roof Ball and Lauren's loving brother had flung her flip-flops off the roof.

For Roof Ball, one person stands on the roof—the old cottage, with its gently sloping roof, was perfect—and the other people stand on the deck on either side of the cottage. Someone pitched the ball up to the person on the roof, who hit it with an oversized plastic yellow bat. The game was always played at dusk, and it became more and more of a challenge to find a lost ball the darker it grew. For some reason, Roof Ball was always accompanied by Donovan singing at top volume on the stereo. You know, "Mellow Yellow," "Season of the Witch," "Atlantis," and my favourite, "There Is a Mountain."

The kids, including any friends they had over, knew all these old songs because we played them so often, so they'd be singing along and whacking the plastic ball with the plastic bat and laughing at one another with crazy abandon. It was a wild game, and no parents or small children were ever invited to play.

Once Donovan was finished the kids would run down to the dock for a swim. The sun would have set by then, and maybe the stars would be out, maybe a couple of bats or fly-ing squirrels. The screech owls would be starting up over on Fairylands, but they'd be drowned out by the noise of splash-ing and laughing and carrying on.

I'd turn off the stereo but always forget to lower the

volume, so that the next day, if I put Harry Manx on, I'd get a shock of sound from the speakers. I'd jump out of my skin, shedding my old complacent self for one split-second, and then resume my usual shape.

Ben went back to the city to find our hot water heater had stopped working. Danielle, who was living in the house for the summer, said it had just stopped that day. He called me to find out what to do.

"Call Enbridge," I said. "It belongs to them and they'll send someone out to look at it."

"Where do I find their number? Do you know our account number? Will someone have to be at home?"

"Look in my files. You'll find a bill there. Yes, someone will have to be at home." Good grief.

Danielle stayed home to let in the man from Enbridge. He said the heater was irreparably broken, and was twenty-five years old and inefficient besides.

Ben called that night. "He couldn't install a new one because we need a new kind of flue or something. They have to come back tomorrow. Danielle has to stay home again. It's a pain in the ass."

"Oh," was all I could muster. I'd be damned if I apologized for not being there to deal with this crisis. He'd dealt with the tree limb and he could deal with this. I didn't begrudge Ben's lack of expertise in coping with household troubles, but it was an eye-opener for me to realize how heavily he relied on me. I was sure he'd be able to do all this without my help, just as he was able to deal with problems at the store, but he wasn't as confident. I couldn't help but feel he resented me not being there.

BEN CALLED TO SAY he was coming up on Saturday night after work, but to go ahead and have dinner without him. We waited anyway, all eleven of us. I decided I had to make an effort to show Ben that I didn't blame him for my pain, since he still insisted on taking responsibility for the accident, so I went with Yeats to pick him up, even though I was still feeling far from spry. Yeats preferred to drive the smaller of our boats, the Scout, and the little boys wanted to come, so the four of us went together, wind in our hair.

I could tell Ben was irked by the smaller boat and by all the people in it — there was barely room for him and his stuff. I sat very still, holding my shoulder as we bumped over the waves, and I told myself Ben would have noticed if I hadn't come.

He said, "Sorry. You didn't need to come."

"Yes, I did. What are you sorry about?"

"Your shoulder. You coming to get me."

"You don't need to be sorry. It's not your fault. Really Ben, look at me. It's. Not. Your. Fault."

He grunted.

"We haven't had dinner yet," I said.

"I'm not hungry. You go ahead."

"You can come over and just sit there. There's a place for you."

He didn't respond.

Greg had made a delicious chickpea curry with rice for dinner. Ben didn't eat and I knew better (we all did) than to try to get him to eat when he didn't want to. He also didn't have any of the banana-blackberry cake that Laurie had made, even though he brought a coffee over with him so he could sit at the table and not talk.

He didn't really say much for the whole weekend. I was exhausted and weepy and didn't want to make love. He didn't even mention it. Two weekends in a row were like this— almost no conversation, profuse apologies, guilt, guilt, guilt.

I could have screamed, but I was trying to stay calm and patient to heal the shoulder. I was in too much physical pain to deal with this emotional stuff.

The weather changed at the end of August, mirroring what was going on inside me: gusty wind high in the trees, rain and thunderstorms, gloom.

Laurie said, "I'm sad today. This always happens at the end of the summer, but it's worse this year."

"Nothing feels right," I said. "I don't want to go back to the city. I'm afraid I won't be able to look after myself, let alone the family."

"Ben and Yeats will have to do it. They'll look after you, won't they?"

"They'll try. But Ben gets so busy. And who knows how much time Yeats will be spending at school? I'm sure glad he decided to stay in Toronto, though. At least he'll be able to do the laundry and clean the kitchen..."

"And Ben will cook you dinner. And I'll come to take you grocery shopping and your shoulder will be better soon, anyway."

"I feel so helpless, so useless. I can't do anything without this pain shooting into my shoulder. I'm tired of it. I don't know if I'll be able to work, but I'm going to try. "

"Maybe you should give it more time."

"I don't want to give it more time. And I don't want to go home, either. I don't know what I want, except for this pain to go away."

Every day, my journal started the same way: *A bad, restless night. I kept waking up in a painful position.* I woke five or six times a night. Some nights I didn't sleep at all, despite the rain on the roof and the wind in the pines.

Ben drove all my family over to the mainland, but because university didn't start until the following week, the three of us stayed at the cottage alone together. It was very quiet on the lake. No dogs barking or doors slamming on neighbouring islands, no jet-skis roaring past or little people running over to our cottage asking for Ben's baking. It was restful and my guys took care of me, but the shoulder wasn't mending. I was living on Advil and ice and whatever healing vibes the forest sent me, but the pain wouldn't abate.

I SAT ON THE front verandah with a glass of wine, breathing in the city. Danielle was back at Western and all the boys had started university. The city was green and lush and not too noisy, but it was the *city* and I didn't want to be there. Ben was in the kitchen making dinner and Yeats was upstairs listening to Townes Van Zandt. I could hear the music through his open window, hear the regret and heartbreak in Townes's voice as he sang of the lonesome blue jay and the crying cuckoo.

We sold books at Michael Ondaatje's launch of *The Cat's Table*, at a restaurant in the west end. I sat at the table, hoping the credit card machine didn't hurt my shoulder. We used the old-fashioned imprinters and every time I pushed the top part over the bottom, my shoulder cried out. It was no good, but I worked anyway because it was busy and I didn't want to let Ben down.

Rupert came in from another event and spelled me off. I left the table and mingled, careful to avoid shaking anyone's hand. I was beginning to learn which actions caused what kind of pain.

After this event I went see my doctor. I'd been going to the physiotherapist and doing exercises, icing the shoulder and taking Advil, but it was only getting worse. The shoulder felt stiff and sore all the time, getting stiffer and sorer by the day.

My doctor asked me to raise my arm at different angles and when I couldn't raise it more than six inches in any direction, she said, "You have Frozen Shoulder, Lynn."

"Frozen Shoulder? What's that?"

She looked regretful as she said, "It's an inflammation of the joint capsule. And chronic spasm of the surrounding muscles. It might get a bit worse before it starts to get better.

You can have a cortisone injection right into the joint, but we have to combine that with an ultrasound to make sure we're hitting the exact spot. There are possible complications with that. You can think about it."

I was wondering about the look on her face. I said, "How long does it take to get better?"

"Back to full range of motion and strength? Typically, eighteen months."

"*What?* Eighteen *months?*"

She nodded and we sat in silence for a few seconds. I could hardly breathe.

"Okay," I said slowly, "and if I don't have the injection, how long before this *pain* goes away?"

"Well, that varies. Probably four to eight weeks for the worst of the inflammation to go down, but yours was caused by trauma, so it's hard to say."

"So that means I need to tell Ben to hire someone else to work through Christmas?"

She watched while I started to cry and then handed me a tissue.

"It would heal faster if you could do nothing, really, except work on this. Physio, ultrasound, acupuncture, massage, ice. I'll give you a prescription for anti-inflammatories and Tylenol 3s." I had told her I wasn't sleeping. "The Tylenol is for night-time, so you can sleep. But they might constipate you, so beware."

She gave me a gentle hug before leaving the room and I felt wretched. Eighteen months? It couldn't be true.

Over the next few weeks I learned that several of my girlfriends had had frozen shoulder, one of them three separate times. She'd had the cortisone shot each time. Another friend had opted not to have the shot and said she had three or four weeks of intense pain before it lessened. Her sister had had it, too. My neighbour had frozen shoulder one time when she was younger. One of the shopkeepers on the Danforth had had it in both shoulders at the same time (it could always be worse, right?). Everywhere I went, I met more and more people who had had this ailment I'd never heard of before.

I couldn't work or drive or write or chop vegetables. I couldn't do anything with my right arm, my dominant arm. I couldn't exercise beyond walking and even then I had to be mindful not to jar the arm. I ate and brushed my hair with my left arm. Since I was the person who usually did just about everything around the house, from grocery shopping to laundry, from grinding the coffee to feeding the cat, the family quickly had to adjust. Ben loved to cook and now he did the shopping as well, but we were approaching the busy time of year in the store. I was a bit panicked at the thought of asking my guys to do everything, even though they quite cheerfully offered.

I was resolute about continuing with my weekly writing group, but had to write with my left hand. I had some experience doing this because every week we did a ten-minute writing exercise using our non-dominant hand. I liked those sessions because they seemed to access a different part of my creative brain, but it was slow going and doing it for the entire morning was tiring.

Everything made my shoulder scream in pain. It turned out I was part of the small percentage of people who are stimulated by codeine, so the Tylenol 3s were a failure. The pain subsided but I was wide awake nearly all night. I tried taking them for three consecutive nights, just in case, but was then so badly constipated that I gave up and stuffed the bottle of pills deep into my underwear drawer.

It felt like I was under notice from the universe to slow right down. It was time to stop doing all the most important things I'd taken for granted—work, writing, exercise, sleep—and figure out who I was once these aspects of my life were taken away. It was time to reconsider everything.

YEATS PLEDGED TO HELP me around the house while I was recovering. One thing he couldn't do, though, was drive, and even this situation didn't inspire him to get his license. But he took out the garbage, raked the leaves, did laundry, carried groceries. I realized that although he and Ben often helped out with these chores and others around the house, I had largely kept responsibility of them. I loved raking the leaves and shovelling the snow and walking out to the Danforth to grocery shop. I didn't want to let it all go and I wondered if Ben would be happy doing *all* the driving.

"I love being your chauffeur, baby," he said.

I was in such an exhausted snit that even that didn't cheer me up.

I had to be mindful about everything I did and it was

draining. I may have thought that a decade of meditation and fourteen years of yoga had prepared me for just sitting there, but this was really hard-core Zen practise and I fought it all the way. I was miserable. I was focused on what I couldn't do, rather than on what this accident was offering me — time to reconsider my life.

Then, one morning I sat in bed and decided I had to surrender to it, like the Lama of Shey Gompa. No more craving what I couldn't do. I remembered how, when Yeats was a newborn and I was crying on the phone to my midwife, she said, "The only way to survive this with any joy is to surrender to it. Surrender to your baby."

Her words were like magic: a little shift of mind, and a whole new life opened up. So I sat on the bed remembering that shift and cried a little with relief. I could surrender to this, too.

I surrendered to the immobility and to months of physio and pain and a feeling of uselessness. I surrendered to Ben, asking him to tie my hair back so I could take a shower, opening every single door for me, and doing up my zippers and making my breakfast. I surrendered to the goddess of the household, who told me (in the form of my imagination) that it was okay to let the house go for now. I gave myself permission to not care about stacks of papers and magazines, or boots and shoes in a messy heap at the front door.

It took a while but eventually I found that when I gave myself permission to do "nothing," I set myself free in a profound way. I realized that it was like birdwatching. It may look like I was out there doing something—looking for birds—but really I was just giving myself the gift of freedom. I was not coming back with anything tangible (maybe a story or two) and, for the most part, the time I spent outdoors was experienced, at the most profound level, internally.

Throughout those months of immobile self-awareness, I learned that all those things I thought were important to me really *were* important. I wanted to get back to the bookstore, I wanted to get back to writing, and I wanted to get back to exercising and keeping house (although I admit I was very happy to give up a lot of the chores). I also learned that I didn't mind if Ben did all the driving.

I usually drove us everywhere, including up to the cottage. Now Ben drove and I sat behind him so the seatbelt didn't dig into the front of my right shoulder. Yeats sat in the passenger seat and chose the music.

Because I was sitting behind Ben, I didn't feel the need to converse with him, or with anyone at all. It was perfect. I could look out the window and daydream, something I had always done as a child on family holidays.

I saw things that I'd never noticed in all the years of being focused on the road ahead. On Highway 118 out of Port Carling, the trees along the road were a thin curtain hiding all sorts of development. I'd always thought it was thick forest. On Highway 400 I saw the same thing and I saw quarries, too, where I used to think there were fields. In the city, I noticed alleyways and gardens and architectural details I'd never seen before. I found myself looking out the car window as we passed buildings and marvelling at the stonework or the rooflines.

My world was changing around me.

WE SPENT OUR LAST cottage weekend of the year on Thanksgiving. I still couldn't do a thing, so I managed to get out of almost all the housework, including cooking the big dinner.

Mom or Laurie always cooked the turkey (which the three of us didn't eat anyway, being vegetarians), and I provided a few of the vegetables along with a tofu dish. This year my family excused us from any cooking. Ben prepared a Brussels sprout salad since that's one of his specialties, but that was it. We gathered in the new cottage, where the children made a centrepiece from colourful gourds and red and yellow leaves they'd collected from the woods. We lit candles, drank good wine, and were surrounded by the smell of pumpkin pie.

Thanksgiving at the cottage was always bittersweet, because it marked the end of the summer and the onset of winter, when our families didn't see much of one another. I found myself mourning the passing of summer at Thanksgiving, but the deciduous trees were beautiful with their changing colours and the air was fresh and cool.

There was much to be done to close up the cottages and I couldn't do any of it. Ben cleaned out the fridge at the old cottage; he vacuumed all the carpets, swept and mopped the bathroom and kitchen floors. He folded the sheets and towels and packed up the food to bring home. He and Yeats took the stereo apart and packed it into the back closet.

"Thanks, Ben," I said to him, over and over again, until finally he said, "Stop it. You've done all this stuff for twenty years." Oh yeah. I have.

Meanwhile, Yeats helped with the outdoor chores — he piled the floaty toys into a room at the boathouse, moved the dock and deck furniture inside, put up the storm windows on the screened-in porch, brought in the beach toys and the path lights. Suddenly, it occurred to me that these men in my life were cheerfully doing everything *because* I couldn't do anything. It made them feel good. I also realized that normally I took on way too much, when it seemed I didn't even need to supervise.

We visited all our special places on the island before leaving for the winter. I went with Laurie and Greg to the main dock to watch the play of light over the lake, and then with Ben to sit on the rock at the beach. Then everyone came together at the new dock to watch the children have one last, freezing, jump in the water. We listed all of the things we saw, year in, year out.

All summer long, we spoke in singulars: "I saw the loon this morning." Or, "It's been a while since we saw the hummingbird." Our cottage life had its own world of archetypes. We went down to the beach and sat on Family Rock, heard the kingfisher out in the bay. If we adjusted our vision, maybe we'd see it hovering for a few seconds before it plunged into the lake. The heron flew past, feet dragging behind. We sighed at the abundance, sunlight on the water, our sense of wonder deepening bird by bird.

I saw the loon that last weekend off the north dock. It had its winter plumage on, so it wasn't recognizable to my sister-in-law, who was standing beside me. She was surprised to hear of winter plumage and I took a moment to marvel at all the things there were to know.

We saw only one raven over Thanksgiving weekend. Our archetypal Raven, bidding us farewell for the season, farewell for the year.

I spent Monday afternoon looking everywhere for Pippin, who was in hiding since he knew we were leaving and he hated being in his carrying cage. He finally materialized from under the deck, but only after I'd stopped looking for him. He meowed at me and I scooped him up, wincing with the weight of him pulling my shoulder. This was one chore no one else would attempt for fear of being bitten and scratched — the picking up of the cat. I dumped him in one of the back bedrooms and shut the door.

Greg drove us back to the mainland later that afternoon with his boys tagging along for the ride.

Taylor asked, "What would you have done if you couldn't find Pippin?"

"I don't know, Taylor. We couldn't really leave him here for the winter."

"He'd freeze!" yelled Noah.

"He'd starve!" yelled Taylor.

"We wouldn't leave him," said Yeats. "We'd stay until he

appeared, just like he always does."

"He's part of the family," Greg said. "I hope your shoulder gets better soon, Lynn. How are you going to wrap Christmas presents?"

I looked at Yeats, who said, "I'll do it."

BACK IN THE CITY, Ben left the house at 8:30 every morning and wasn't home until after 11 p.m., working at the store and at the International Festival of Authors. I had to face the fact that until the end of November, he'd be home, on average, only two nights a week. It was his busiest time and I wouldn't be working with him. It turned out my old joke was true: if I didn't work with him, I'd never see him.

Ben even missed Yeats's high school graduation ceremony, and I was in no mood to understand.

"What do you mean you have to work?" I said. "Can't you get someone else to work for even just a couple of hours? I'm sure you could if you wanted to."

"I have to work that night. Rupert and Titus are both working, too, and Andrea, but we need two people at each side. Yeats said he doesn't mind."

Yeats said to me, "I don't even want to go, Mom. Why should I go? They'll send me my diploma in the mail if I don't go."

I was appalled and I wondered for a minute if this was really all about my own needs and expectations. But I said what I was thinking anyway. "I'd really like to see you graduate, after all that work." (Mine or his?) "After all *your* work. It'll be fun, too, and you can introduce me to some of your friends afterwards."

"I guess."

We weren't spending much time together, any of us, and the IFOA only made that worse. I was barely involved in their lives since I was so focused on trying to mend, and I felt a pressing need to attend Yeats's graduation. He finally agreed to go, but Ben couldn't be swayed.

It turned out there was a publisher's party that night that Ben wanted to go to, even after working until ten o'clock. Well. I decided that was a rotten choice, but I was so emotionally charged I didn't trust myself to speak. I went over and over it in my head, but there was no spin I could put on it where it came out okay to miss your child's graduation, even if the child didn't care. I didn't say anything out loud, but I let the anger fester inside me.

IN THE JARVIS COLLEGIATE auditorium I sat in the third row to the left of the stage, next to a sweet and very old Asian gentleman who spoke little English. He smiled and nodded at me and told me he was there to watch his granddaughter graduate. The students filled the centre section of the hall and a small orchestra played in front of the stage. On stage sat staff and school board personnel, along with members of the student council. Once the audience was assembled, the emcee introduced the first speaker, the principal, and on went the show: the speeches, the awards, and then the handing out of the diplomas.

When his granddaughter crossed the stage the man beside me tapped my arm and said, "That's her. See how beautiful!"

He was beaming and crying just a bit, which made me teary, too. I really teared up when Yeats received his diploma and I pointed him out to my new friend. I thought of all the hours I'd spent coaxing Yeats through school, all the drama and angst, all the nights I stayed up late trying to calm him down, get him through life. This part of the journey was completed, thank goodness, and I was here to witness this milestone.

When the ceremony was over, the old man opened the programme to the last page and asked for my autograph. It was a strangely intimate moment and I was filled with confusion. I wanted to say, "But I'm not famous." Instead, I nodded and smiled at him and signed my name. He asked me to put down my son's name, too.

I was brimming with pride and something like relief that Yeats had achieved this goal. He'd made the honour roll, he'd received an award for Writer's Craft, and he'd been accepted to all three universities to which he applied. In my heart I'd known it would be this way, but I remembered, too, all that anxiety, all the time we'd spent together trying to sort out why school was a good idea.

We went to the reception in the cafeteria and I watched Yeats socialize with his classmates. He introduced me to some of them but mostly I kept a distance and just watched.

He was expansive and open, hugging some of the girls and high-fiving the boys. He laughed and talked and appeared totally relaxed. I chatted with a couple of teachers, who had only good things to say about my boy. While I talked with one of his English teachers, Yeats came up to us.

The teacher said, "Congratulations, Yeats. You've done a great job in high school."

"Thanks," Yeats said.

"Are you going to work in the bookshop for the summer?"

"A bit. I'll be doing some birdwatching, too, and spending some time at the cottage. What are you doing this summer?"

I looked at Yeats and marvelled once again at how unreserved he was in public. This boy who has no trouble showing me all his fears and frustrations brings a cheerful, open grace to face the world.

I wondered how surprised Yeats's teachers would be to discover his depth of loathing for school, since his public persona was so agreeable. They were happy to hear he'd decided to go to the University of Toronto, and the teachers who remembered Rupert were equally happy to hear he was going to school in the fall, too. Both boys were enrolled at St. Michael's College downtown. I was hoping they'd inspire one another.

Yeats didn't want to stay very late, so we left the school and waited outside for the bus. It was a blustery Friday night at the end of October.

"I'm proud of you," I said to him, at the risk of inducing annoyance.

But he smiled, looking shy for a moment. Then he said, "Thanks, Mom. Thanks for everything."

THIRTEEN

BEN CAME BIRDWATCHING WITH Yeats and me the following May, down to Point Pelee for the 2012 spring migration. He hadn't come with us to Pelee before because he was too busy but also because he thought it was our thing, not his, and he wasn't sure about the entire endeavour. He came this time because I still couldn't drive and because he knew we needed to spend some time together.

When I thought back to the fall and all the pain I was in, and how hard it was to sleep, and how much Ben was working, it was little wonder to me that our marriage had reached an edge. My journals from that time are page after page of the therapies I was having—physio, acupuncture, massage, homeopathy—as well as a good deal of moaning. Five months in the life of a long marriage may not seem like much, but two busy people often wind up taking one another for granted, or they don't tend the marriage as they ought. I suddenly wasn't busy at all, except for tending to myself. Everything was off-kilter.

Ben and I loved one another, but my injury highlighted the weak spots in our relationship. I suppose that was the silver lining, because we were both devoted to making it strong again.

Over breakfast one Sunday in January I'd said to Ben, "Yeats is disappointed that we won't be going to Pelee this year."

Ben said, "Why won't you?"

"I'm not sure I'll be able to drive by then." I still couldn't brush my hair using my right arm and the mere thought of putting the car in gear made the shoulder flare up.

"Well, then," he said, "I'll have to do it. I'll be your driver."

I looked hard at him to see if he thought I'd tried to manipulate him into being our chauffeur. I hadn't even thought of Ben driving down, of him coming birdwatching with us on three of our most intensive days of the year.

"Are you sure?" I said.

"Yeah, why?"

"It's far. It's a long drive. It's a lot of walking and we get up at 5:30 in the morning and it might be pouring rain."

"So?" He looked at me over the table. Thin winter sun was pouring in through the bow window, illuminating everything, making us a little bit warmer. He said, "This has been a hard time for you. I love you like crazy and I want to do something for you. I work all the time. The store has been great, but it's a lot of work and I'm always gone." I was nodding and trying not to cry. "It's okay," he said.

It was okay. I said, "Thanks, Ben. I'm sorry, too. This shoulder thing. I've felt a million miles away from you."

We both nodded and looked one another in the eyes, and I saw that gentle sweetness that lies at the core of my husband. I thought, *This is why I'm with this man.*

"Thanks," I said again. "We'd love to have you drive us."

Yeats and I had our rhythm together when we bird-watched, though. We had certain music we liked to listen to in the car, we had our walking pace, and we hardly spoke on the path. I was happy to eat lentil roll-ups for lunch and dinner, three days straight if it came to that. When I told Yeats that we *would* go to Pelee because his father was coming along, he was a bit conflicted. Honestly, I was, too.

Ben said, "I'm just the driver. You guys do what you always do and I'll do it with you. Just tell me."

Yeats was most nervous about the music in the car, something that totally confounded Ben. He said he'd listen to anything, but Yeats and I had heard years and years of Ben groaning about particular bands. Yeats didn't trust that Ben wouldn't say something disparaging about a band he loved, which made him wary. I explained all this to Ben, who stared at me in disbelief. His outspoken ways had come back to haunt him, but we loved him for his outspokenness, too.

THE BIRD MIGRATION WEEKEND at Pelee coincided with Mother's Day, but I'd never been big on breakfast in bed, and besides, I'd spent the past couple of Mother's Days birding as well. It seemed somehow fitting, watching birds migrate in order to nest while contemplating motherhood myself.

On our way down to Pelee, we stopped again at Wheatley Provincial Park. It was such a quiet place and we wanted to share it with Ben. As before, we saw no one on our walk through the forest and around the pond. We saw a few birds—a house wren, a few chestnut-sided warblers, an ovenbird, some northern flickers—and on our way back to the car we saw some wood ducks and northern shovelers. All told, we saw thirteen species at Wheatley, which wasn't great. Ben lived up to his promise to be "just the chauffeur." He didn't try to set the pace in the forest or tell us where he thought we should go. He let us do our usual thing and tagged along behind. We were happy to have him there and, as often as I thought seemly, I'd grab his arm and give him a quick kiss in appreciation.

It isn't far from Wheatley to Leamington, maybe ten kilometres. We passed fields full of fruit trees and greenhouses, roadside stands selling asparagus and apple cider, and then the gas stations and car lots that announced modern civilization.

We checked into our motel in Leamington—a different one from last time—and drove straight out to the park. It was only about four in the afternoon, and we thought we might as well start birding right away.

Not far into the park, just past the first information area, we saw a small cluster of people on the road, looking through their binoculars. We found an illegal but safe place to park the car and walked back to join the group. It was the same spot where the great horned owls had been nesting last year, but this year we saw them clearly. Two of them were looking out at the dozen people looking into the forest at them. They were big and solid-looking, and all three of us stood in awe before them.

More often than not, when Yeats asked me what I'd most like to see before we set out birding, my answer was owls. I wanted to see all our owls, not so I could check them off my life-list (if I'd kept one), but so I could experience the charge I feel each time I see a new one. Owls are still and predatory. They are a little bit scary, even to a human many times their size. They sit and stare and seem to belong so profoundly to where they are, to the forest and the earth, that I feel like bowing down before them.

Every once in a while at the cottage, I'll be wakened in the night by a barred owl. They're the ones that call, *Whoo-hoo! Whoo-hoo!* or, *Who cooks for you? Who cooks for you?* Sometimes, before making this iconic call, they'll let go a blood-curdling scream. I'll sit bolt upright in bed, heart pounding, eyes trying desperately to see in the pitch dark. *Who screamed? Who's in trouble?* Then I'll hear the hooting and I'll sigh, able to lie back down and relax. *It's that owl.*

So we looked at these owls on Point Pelee for a while, then went back to the car and moved on down the track.

We parked at the Blue Heron area and walked onto the

boardwalk, out into the marsh. Ben said he was surprised by how few people there were. He was expecting more, based on what we'd said. I looked around and saw a dozen or so groups of two or three people, everyone slowly making their way around the marsh. We had chosen to walk clockwise when everyone else was going counter-clockwise. It did feel like a lot of people to Yeats and me, who were used to birding practically alone, but we didn't complain. This was Pelee on the busiest migration weekend of the year. *Besides,* I thought, *it will be busier tomorrow morning.*

On the boardwalk that afternoon, we saw common yellowthroats and black terns, as well as various turtles and dragonflies. Blue herons flew past in the distance and turkey vultures high above. In the woods by the parking lot, we saw a rose-breasted grosbeak, white-crowned and white-throated sparrows, a yellow warbler, and a grey catbird. Again, it was a short list, but we were hopeful for the morning.

Our motel was not as close to the park this time, but it was far nicer than last year's. The three of us shared a room: two queen-sized beds, and a little fridge that we crammed full of food. The motel offered breakfast starting at 4:30 for avid birders, but that first morning Ben and I went down to eat at six. We weren't as keen as in previous years, and Yeats was cool with that. He seemed to need more sleep these days and had become, I was happy to note, more practical than fanatical in his birding habits.

The serve-yourself breakfast was awful, not at all up to my obsessively health-conscious standards: white bread, white bagels, syrupy fruit-bottomed yogurt, sugar-based cereals. But the worst part was that everything was served on Styrofoam — plates, bowls, cups for juice and coffee. I didn't fancy drinking toxic styrene chemicals with my breakfast, so I forewent coffee.

Yeats and I always stood out among other birders and so did Ben. I was wearing a pair of light-blue cotton pants with a T-shirt and a long-sleeved flowered shirt buttoned on top, along with my walking shoes. Yeats and Ben both wore shorts and T-shirts with their New Balance running shoes. Not that either of them ever went running.

Everyone else in the breakfast room was dressed in gear that came straight from an outdoors outfitter — khaki-coloured pants and shirts made from one of those high-tech breathable fabrics and with multiple pockets for storing things; sensible hiking shoes; brimmed hats with strings so if a gust of wind came along, the hat wouldn't fly away. We had our baseball caps.

Every time Yeats and I were among other birders, they stared at us. We didn't mind. Ben, the old hippie, didn't even notice.

We drove straight to the information centre, where we parked among the three hundred or more cars already there. We ran into Donna, a friend from Toronto who was an avid birder and who was there with a friend. We made introductions in the parking lot and then went our separate ways. They were headed right for the tip and we were off into the forest behind the centre.

We joked that we saw someone we knew everywhere we went. Usually it was someone Ben knew through bookselling (which was the case with Donna); but out here in bird land, we might expect to see people from other parts of our life.

There were more people and fewer birds on the forest trail this year. We walked slowly, stopping frequently to look out into the woods, so several groups overtook us. Most people smiled or nodded hello. Most people were being very quiet.

The list of what we saw that morning looked something like this: red-eyed vireo, great crested flycatcher, scarlet tanager, Baltimore oriole, American redstart, cedar waxwing, chipping sparrow. We also saw four or five different warblers — including the elusive prothonotary.

I have to admit that it wasn't as exciting to see this little yellow bird this year. Yeats was nearly blasé — it wasn't a first sighting, after all. And there were more people around, big men with long-lens cameras setting up their tripods, taking up a lot of space on the trail. I didn't find them irritating, exactly — they had as much right to be there as we did — but I wished they weren't so big. The birds they were trying to photograph with their giant equipment were so small. The men were dressed all in black and khaki. These little birds were yellow and light grey. I looked from one to the other. I knew that one of these guys might take a photograph that would end up in a birding magazine and that a child somewhere might see it and be turned on to birding. Things like that happened. But they were taking up so much room!

We went into the information centre and bought Yeats a hat. I bought a giant granola cookie and outside we bought coffee and a snack for Ben. The coffee was in cups made from recycled paper. There was no Styrofoam or plastic in sight.

We decided to take the next shuttle bus to the tip of Pelee, not because we were hopeful of seeing many birds there, but because we couldn't bear the thought of Ben coming all the way here and not seeing the southernmost tip of Canada.

The tip was very crowded, just like last year. It was a bit unpleasant, and I wondered if it would have been different if we'd come out here at 5:30 a.m. instead of 8:30 a.m. Possibly, but I wouldn't have been surprised to find as many fanatical birders out here at that time of day. The largest flocks of birds flew over the lake at night, when no one was allowed in the park, but maybe some flocks flew early in the morning. Maybe it was worth it to get up at 4:30 and be here for that. It would be amazing to see huge flocks of birds.

We wandered around for half an hour. There were a lot of people also wandering around. There were groups with guides, all clustered together and looking up at, say, a red-headed woodpecker. A lot of people were talking.

We walked down the beach towards the very tip of Pelee but didn't go out onto the sand. The beach was a different shape than it had been last year, and there were signs everywhere warning people not to swim, that the currents off the tip were swift and dangerous. It was a continually changing landscape.

We tired of the crowds and took the next bus back to our

car. We saw two wild turkeys on the bus ride back. People pointed. Turkeys are like swans; they're so big that on first sight, they're startling. Can they really be birds? And why do people eat turkey and not swan? Someone who has eaten swan can let me know.

Our next stop along the point was the DeLaurier Homestead area. We circumnavigated the old farmhouse, looking for birds as we went. Some people were having a picnic. Others were standing around waiting for their tour to start. We headed off down one of the trails into the woods and finally started to see some birds.

We saw the gorgeous male indigo bunting. It's as blue as the cardinal is red, a spectacular sight. Like other blue birds, this bunting's feathers lack blue pigment. Instead, its colour comes from microscopic structures in the makeup of its feathers, which reflect and refract blue light. It seems like a trick, a bit of sorcery, since these birds do look so blue.

We saw several groups of various warblers: Wilson's, magnolia, Blackburnian, yellow, bay-breasted. Warblers spend their time on the go, flitting from branch to branch eating bugs. No sooner did I get one in my binocular-sight than it was gone. You had to know your warblers ahead of time in order to identify them in the field. You had to know, for example, that the Wilson's warbler has no streaking on its breast, while the Canada warbler has a lovely necklace of jet stripes; otherwise, you might not be able to tell them apart. Among some of the warblers, the variations are small, especially among some of the females. Some of the female warblers even look like other species, such as the female house finch, except that the finch is smaller and has a different beak.

The point is, you had to be ready. You needed to be someone like Yeats, who spent hours and hours with the bird books, absorbing the minute differences, memorizing the similarities.

I remember one day asking him what he was doing as he lounged on his bed at home. "Memorizing the flycatchers." Which, by the way, is impossible to do since two of them — the alder and the willow — are exactly alike except for their song. Until the 1970s, these two birds were considered one species and so, in order to decide which one you're looking at in the field, you have to hear it sing.

I was not like Yeats, who memorized the birds, but I was with Yeats. Ben and I both had the benefit of our son's ency-clopaedic knowledge and ability to identify birds. Without him, we would not have been in the woods on Point Pelee on a beautiful spring morning. We would have been in the city selling books.

We came upon a group of about twenty-five people clus-tered together. All of them were looking up. We figured they must have spotted something good up in those trees so we joined them.

I asked the woman in front of me what they were look-ing at, and she said it was an eastern screech owl, red morph. Eastern screech owls come in two colours — red and grey — which scientists call "morphs." Another owl! Two different owl species in one weekend! I asked her where it was and she pointed up at a tall tree not too far away.

"It's impossible to see, it's so well camouflaged," she said. "But if you watch where those warblers are dive-bombing, then look through your binoculars, you'll get it."

Yeats was standing behind me and said, "Yes! There it is!"

I did as the woman suggested. There were five or six warblers acting crazy, repeatedly flying right at the tree and then swerving sharply away. They obviously wanted the owl gone. I found it through the binoculars quite easily once I knew where to look.

I'd seen these small owls while kayaking around Fairy-lands, and one night there were two of them on our island — but I could see them only in silhouette, high in the pines.

This was a clear sighting. This owl was less than half the size of the great horned. It had tucked itself into a V in the tree and blended right in, colours exact. None of these people would have seen it if it hadn't been for the aggravated warblers.

I offered Ben my binoculars but he shrugged them off as usual. He found them awkward with his glasses. He didn't seem to have the same need as we did to see every single bird.

We kept walking and followed a path that took us along-side some canals that led out to the lake. We sat on a bench on a flat little bridge over one of these canals and watched a beaver swim towards us and right under the bridge. The canal stretched as far as we could see, woodland thick on either side like walls, birdsong the only sound. We could have been the last three people on Earth.

We found a segment of road in the forest. It bisected a trail and had been left to tell a story. There were benches and some information boards, some with flora and fauna, others with old photographs of the road. This road used to stretch from farm to farm. This whole area, now a forest, was farmland. Most of the road, as well as the farms and all the buildings, had been dismantled and taken away. Nature, and nature tourism, had claimed it.

While we sat and rested on the benches, we saw a northern parula, a black-throated blue warbler, a blue-grey gnatcatcher, and an eastern towhee — all birds we'd seen before. We waited a while longer to see if anything else would come and then set out again. As we were winding our way back to the car, Ben spotted something racing across the forest floor.

"Look! What is it? A mink?" It was a small, brown mammal, very low to the ground and running like heck. In its mouth flopped a dead rabbit.

Yeats said, "Yes, I think it's a mink. Look at it go!" The animal zigged and zagged, running back and forth across a creek, dragging its prey, which was just about as big as it was. Finally, it made a dash in a straight line and dived into an old tree stump.

"That was fantastic," Ben said. "Just as exciting as seeing birds."

In all, we saw about sixty-eight species of birds that day. We were happy with that, but decided to drive back to the boardwalk at the Blue Heron area to see the black terns again.

Maybe we'd see something else. We'd given up on seeing as many as we had the year before.

We parked at the Blue Heron area again and Yeats went into the woods first, as usual. Not five steps from the car he said, "Look! A snake!"

He gestured up with his eyes, and then raised his binoculars. Ben and I looked up to the top of a dead tree where a very large snake was slithering slowly into a hole. And then it was gone.

"It's a fox snake," said Yeats. "That was great!" Then he bounded down the path.

Ben looked at me and said, "How did he see that?"

I smiled. "He's good."

Ben shook his head. "If we'd been ten seconds later, we would have missed it. That was amazing!"

I think that snake was the highlight of Ben's day. It was an eastern fox snake, the second-largest snake in Ontario (after the eastern rat snake). The eastern fox snake usually grows to about one metre long. We didn't know how long this one was since we didn't see it enter the tree, but we saw over half a metre disappear into that hole, which made it the biggest wild snake I'd ever seen. The eastern fox snake is listed as "threatened" both in Ontario and nationally. It is a protected species.

We saw the black terns again, only two of them, sweeping and swooping over the marsh. We walked out onto the boardwalk and no matter how far we went, those terns stayed a good distance away. We saw another fox snake, about half the girth of the first. This one was slowly uncoiling and slithering into the reeds, off to find dinner. We saw three different kinds of turtles, and Yeats was sorry he didn't have our reptile and amphibian book because we could only identify one for sure, the painted turtle. He jotted down notes so he could look up the others later.

I said, "Would this be a good reason to get an iPhone or some other internet device?"

Yeats glared at me even though he knew I was kidding. If he wrote down the description, made mental notes, and spent half an hour sorting out which turtles we saw, he'd remember them forever. The next time, he'd know which turtle it was. If he looked them up on the Internet, he wouldn't remember them and he'd always be dependent on the device. Some people might say, "But he'd always have the device so why does it matter?" But having the knowledge is always better than having the ability to look it up. Or is it the same?

For people like Yeats, who have steel-trap memories, it's not the same at all.

THAT NIGHT BEN AND I went out for a nice Italian dinner, while Yeats stayed in to update his lists. We usually ate food we brought from home on our birding jaunts, so this was a treat. I had a glass of wine, also something I never usually did when birding.

I thanked Ben for bringing us down here. He reached across the table for my hand and said, "I love you, Lynn. Thanks for letting me come."

We smiled inanely at one another for a while. Then we started talking about our usual subject: the bookstore. We had a couple of great events coming up and Ben wanted to know if I'd work them.

We had Andrew Motion, who used to be the poet laureate of the UK, coming for a special dinner event.

Ben said, "It's for his novel, but everyone coming to the dinner is a poetry fan. I think we're all hoping he'll recite something."

"Aren't we lucky to be in a business filled with poetry lovers? People who aren't afraid to *say* they read poetry?" I said. "Don't worry, I'll be at that one. And the May Brunch, of course, but I thought the kids were doing most of the events coming up." Ben hosts a monthly "Authors' Brunch" event and has done so since his days at Nicholas Hoare bookstore.

"There are so many of them," Ben sighed. "I have Yeats on a lot. He says he wants to work mostly nights, so that's what he's getting. Rupert is working a lot of nights, too."

"Yeah, Yeats wants to bird-watch during the day, for the migration," I said. "Some mornings all he has to do is lie in bed and watch the tree outside his window. The other morning he counted thirty species in that tree. Not all at once, obviously."

Ben and I laughed. He said, "Rupert's taking that philosophy course in June and then he's off to England in August, and Titus is taking a full course load all summer long. At least Danielle will work. She wants as many shifts as she can get." Rupert had decided to take a Shakespeare course at Oxford, an intensive program that allowed him to get a full credit for one month of classes. He'd go to London and see a play at the Globe Theatre, he'd hang out in libraries and pubs that were hundreds of years old, and he'd meet some new people, too. I was pleased that Rupert was stepping outside his usual circle, getting out of town on his own.

"It's so great having Danielle back. She's a star," I said.

We didn't have to worry about Danielle — she seemed to be grounded and hardworking and managed to stay cheerful on top of that. The boys were always less sure of their next steps and seemed more conflicted. Sometimes I felt like I was holding my breath, waiting for the boys to . . . what? Be satisfied? Settled? There was no such thing as "settled" as far as I could see. You couldn't predict what would throw you off your path or when. And who was I to demand something of these young men that I pushed back against myself? I still didn't have a vision of myself ten years from now. I really only had now.

THE NEXT DAY WE took our own multi-grain bagels down to the breakfast room to toast and then covered them in almond butter, which we'd also brought with us.

Like the year before, we decided to spend Sunday at Hillman's Marsh in the morning and then the rest of the day driving home. Also like last year, there were very few people at the marsh and most of them had congregated at the side closest to the parking lot. They had scopes, which allowed them to see birds from quite a distance. We needed to get closer to the birds, so we walked.

The day was bright but gusty. There was less marsh this year, probably due to the lack of rain we'd experienced that spring, combined with a dearth of snow all winter. Still, there were loads of birds out there: flocks of dunlins and short-billed dowitchers, blue-winged teals and black-bellied plovers. We also saw a green-winged teal for the first time, and a common moor hen.

The green-winged teal is a small duck with distinct colour patterns — iridescent green patches on the wings and a white stripe down the front and, for the males, a green-and-reddish head.

The common moor hen was skulking in some low shrubbery growing along the edge of the marsh. We'd seen something moving in there and we followed it for a couple of minutes. We stood still and then we tried moving quickly, but it stayed in the shrubs. Finally it showed itself and we were rewarded with a new bird. I recognized it immediately from the old bird book, unlike most of the passerines, which are just too similar for me to be able to differentiate between the species. This one was an adult breeding male, with its brilliant red face-shield. That made three brand new birds within five minutes of being at Hillman's Marsh, and our shoes weren't one bit muddy.

As we continued around the marsh we saw various warblers and sparrows and then, finally, we saw *and* heard one of those twin-like flycatchers. Yeats made a positive ID: it was a willow flycatcher. He seemed a bit nonchalant about this sighting, after two years of failing to do it.

He shrugged and said, "I knew I'd get one eventually." My Zen son.

We walked a bit farther along the eastern end of the pond and stopped when we saw a flock flying in the distance. The birds were way up high but coming closer.

Yeats and I raised our binoculars and when they were nearly overhead he said, "Bonaparte's gulls."

There were perhaps two hundred of them, flying in a couple of separate groups. They dropped in altitude and began to circle. They flew around and around in a great, giant circle in the sky, white wings flapping, calls of *kew kew* coming from the flock. We guessed they were feeding up there, and before we had time to wonder aloud at this particular winged waltz, they finished and resumed flying north.

The three of us looked at each other, mirroring one another's awe. Nature was full of split seconds like this, and you needed to be observant to see them.

We felt fuller now, as we walked the rest of the way around the marsh. I certainly did and I could see it on the faces of Ben and Yeats. We were glowing with the circling of those gulls.

Gulls are notoriously difficult to identify. In southern Ontario we have mostly ring-billed and herring gulls. The Sibley guide says of the herring gull: "Variation in its size, structure, and plumage can create confusion with almost every other large gull species." Also, the gulls are famous for inter-breeding, creating hybrid individuals which themselves breed, creating still new hybrids. The smaller gulls are easier to identify, if you know which ones come to your area, but even with those ones, I wouldn't bet my money.

Those had definitely been Bonaparte's gulls, though — they were small and white and had that telltale black head they have in breeding season. There are other small, hooded gulls but of the ones that are mostly white, none come through Pelee, unless they are really off their course. A whole flock wouldn't be off its course. These ones we'd seen were headed off to Northern Ontario to breed and then, in the fall, they'd fly back to the Gulf of Mexico to winter.

Even though it wasn't teeming with rain this year, the wind gusts hadn't let up, and we decided to walk only the short route again. By the time we arrived back at the trail-head, people were approaching and heading off in the direction of the other section of the marsh, which probably had about a thousand birds waiting to be seen. We decided to leave that one for next year since it was already noon and we had a long drive ahead. We were wind-blown and tired from the relentless gale.

Yeats said, "Can we stand in the blind for a few minutes? Maybe something will come."

Ben and I grunted our assent and Yeats stepped up his pace.

But we didn't have to go as far as the blind. A small flock of dunlin appeared, flying wide circles low to the water. They glinted like jewels as they turned in the sun.

The dunlin is a medium-sized sandpiper with a reddish back and long, drooping bill. It breeds in wet, coastal tundra; these ones were probably on their way to Hudson's Bay to nest.

Ben and I were standing together, me leaning against his chest, and Yeats was about three metres away. We were on a grassy laneway between two expanses of marsh, with the wind howling and our hands freezing in our pockets.

Then, it happened in a flash — a flash of birdwing and light, a flash of breath sharply inhaled, a flash of grace. The dunlin had swooped out across the pond and then, seconds later, flown straight towards us. But before they collided with these three people standing still holding their breath, they flew between us. I looked at Yeats and then at Ben, and we all slowly exhaled.

I imagined that I *felt* the birds fly past us, *felt* the small rush of air and the pulse of their wings, but I know I didn't. It had happened too quickly to feel any such sensation. What I felt was this tremendous sense of belonging; that I belonged with these people and on this earth.

None of us spoke for a few seconds and then Ben said, "Holy mackerel! That was unbelievable! They were close enough to touch."

Yeats and I nodded. Yeats turned around and started walking back to the road.

He said over his shoulder, "We don't need to go to the blind anymore."

He was right.

I said to Ben, "Thanks for coming with us this weekend. Thanks for wanting to come."

"Thanks for having me. Happy Mother's Day."

He put his arm around me and we walked like that for a while, watching Yeats stride ahead, his long hair flying in the wind.

FOURTEEN

I WAS WAITING FOR Ben in the car, facing south on Bay Street in front of the store, a Saturday night in May. He was exchanging one set of books for another, unpacking the trunk and filling it up.

We'd spent the day selling books at a symposium on health in the developing world and I was feeling depressed. The problems seemed insurmountable — war, famine, drought. What depressed me even more, though, was our unwitting complicity. A lot of money from our Canada Pension Plan fund to the Teachers' pension plans of every province invested in the manufacture of small arms which made their way to conflicts worldwide and whose sole purpose, let's face it, was to kill people.

And then there was the mining of those rare minerals,

such as coltan, that we needed to run our computers, cell phones, and video game consoles, to make them faster and faster—mining that came with violence and rape. Someone had done the research in the Democratic Republic of the Congo and when they'd laid the map of incidents of violent rape over the map of mining activity, the two corresponded. Seventy percent of the world's mining companies had their headquarters in Canada, including many of those in the DRC.

So I sat thinking about these things and the pit in my stomach got a little bit bigger.

Just then a gull flew down between the buildings, going west along Adelaide Street and looping around in front of the car to fly up and east again, dipping its wings at me.

Not many birds down here, I thought. Saturday night, lots of traffic and city noise. Not many birds, but one seagull, trying to tell me to get on with my life.

YEATS WAS NEARLY NINETEEN now, in his first year of university, and mostly wanted to bird-watch on his own. I offered to go with him to Riverdale Farm, but he gently told me he'd rather go alone.

He looked sad and said, "Sorry, Mom. Riverdale Farm is special to me. I like being alone there." He saw by my face, which I was trying hard to control, that that was not enough of an explanation. He said, "I talk too much when I'm with you."

"We don't have to talk," I said, but he shook his head.

"I want to talk with you. I just want to be alone at the farm. Sorry."

By now I'd arranged my face into a smile and I shrugged, assuring him it was okay and that maybe we'd go to the farm together some other day. Though right then they had baby goats, and I would have liked to see them. *Preferably not by myself,* I thought, but I didn't say that out loud. I was glad that he was independent and I was glad he still lived at home. I knew we'd go birdwatching together again and this thing about the farm was small. Just a momentary heartache that would dissipate as soon as I'd written it down.

Parenting is full of heartaches, some fleeting and some leaving permanent scars.

I had a million memories of being at the farm with Yeats as a youngster and they coalesced into a warm spot deep inside, that same place accessed by the smell of decaying leaves in autumn or the sound of Cat Stevens's "Tea for the Tillerman." I wanted it to go on and on forever, but I knew it couldn't.

One day our final time of birdwatching together will come, but of course we won't know it's the last one. If I thought about that for much longer, I'd be in tears, so I took a long look at that darkness and at my nostalgia, took a deep breath, and let it go.

Sometimes when Yeats went birdwatching alone he had a sadness about him when he set out and I wondered if it was because he was on his own. If he'd rather have a companion, maybe someone who wasn't his mother. A girlfriend. Maybe he'd like to have a girlfriend. But I thought that was just my projecting. I didn't think it was sadness, really. I thought it was just that moment of transition between being in the house where everything was safe and known, and being out in the world where life is unpredictable. He was never the kind of kid who rushed out, seeking the dangerous edge.

IT WAS LATER THAT summer. The three of us stood on the deck at the cottage in the dark, listening to a pair of barred owls calling to one another. The farther one seemed to be on the other side of Fairylands and it made the usual *whoo whowho* call. The closer one was so loud that it may have even been on our island, but we couldn't tell. It also called *whoo whowho*, but added a little descending tremolo at the end: *whoo whowhooooooo*. It sounded like a ghost or a demented opera singer. Each time the birds called, Yeats looked at me, grinning.

We stood out there for five minutes, listening, the dark forest enclosing us but our cozy cottage behind, with its electric light and Pippin sleeping on a chair. The cat didn't bat an eye over these owls. Not much later, though, while we played cards, he raised his head and opened his eyes wide when a dog on Fairylands began to bark. The barking also silenced the owls and we resumed our play.

The next day I watched a raven eviscerate a chipmunk. Ravens seemed to be everywhere; we left some stale crackers on the railing and after they took them, they sat cackling in the pines around the deck. Perhaps they were thanking us, or asking for more.

I heard another raven farther off, making a loud, raspy, repetitive sound. The sound a young bird made when it wanted to be fed. Or the sound of the bungee-jumping toy sheep that Mom brought Yeats home from New Zealand years ago, a deranged *Waaaaaa*.

I found the bird in my binoculars. An adult raven was sitting on a high branch, feeding bits of chipmunk to its young one, who was making all the noise. I watched as the bird pecked and pecked at the chipmunk, which lay flung out upside down on the branch, its throat exposed and its belly being torn out by the raven. Ravenous.

The only time the young raven stopped its mesmerizing sound was when its parent stuffed a piece of meat into its mouth. I watched as the chipmunk's belly grew bloodier and bloodier. I watched as the raven pulled out a piece of intestine that looked just like spaghetti. With its claws clamped tightly on the chipmunk, the bird pulled the intestine upwards as far as it could and then dropped its head down, letting the morsel sag. Then it twisted the sagging bit around in its beak and pulled again. It repeated this action over and over until it had had enough and gave a strong tug to set the flesh free. It had accumulated a good-sized bite, which it fed right into the waiting mouth beside it.

I had seen enough.

I MADE A CUP of tea and took it down to the dock. It was early on a cloudy September morning and no one else was moving. Ben and Yeats were both asleep. The rest of my family was in the city and so were most of the other cottagers at our end of the lake.

The water was flat calm and the sun poked a ray through steely clouds, sending a carpet of jewels spreading from the horizon right to the dock. Two seagulls flew past, a couple of minutes apart, both of them adjusting their path so they could fly right over me. The loon kept calling, calling, calling.

I sat until the dew soaked through the towel I put on the chair and into my pyjamas. I'd drunk half my tea and the rest was cold, along with my feet in their flip-flops. It was time to go back to the cottage, but I couldn't move. I needed to soak up as much of this scene as I could before heading back to Toronto and crashing into my other life — the life of a busy bookseller in a teeming city.

The transition to the city was always difficult, always required a conscious effort to stay balanced. Yeats transitioned now by going birdwatching as many times as he could in his first weeks back. I tried to go for walks, too, just around the neighbourhood, and I always scheduled a visit with at least one good friend.

When Yeats was small we had a really hard time with this transition, neither of us seeing the point in coming back to the city just so he could go to school. There seemed to be so much more to learn in the forest and on the lake. Those were the times when I thought of home-schooling, though that's not the path we took.

Those early days of September, Yeats and I would leave the house a bit ahead of schedule and walk down to the school, stopping along the way to look at flowers and ferns and the occasional bird that caught our eye. It wouldn't be long, I knew, before we'd be back to our normal routine, driving to school because I had to hurry on to something else, plunging back into our homework wars.

I reflected on the changes the years had wrought as I sat alone on the dock that glorious morning. Yeats was in university now and wholly in charge of his assignments; I had my work in the bookshop, my writing group, and friends to look forward to. Our lives were evolving, and Yeats depended on me less to go birdwatching. He went on his own.

AND NOW, WINTER: I peeked out the bedroom window to gauge the day. It was 7 a.m. and the sun wasn't up yet. Grey sky one morning, frost on the balcony railing. Grey sky the next morning, no frost. Ribbons of pink in the eastern sky the next morning and I knew we would have rain or snow.

The sun rose into encroaching clouds, and I had long since dropped the edge of the curtain and gone downstairs to feed the cat.

What happened next in a day? If we were lucky, nothing out of the ordinary. Breakfast, shower, dress. Put the cat out and then let the cat in. Read the front section of the newspaper and note the weather in various spots around the world. −15 in Winnipeg, +30 in Singapore. Imagine for a second being in both of those places at once and spend a minute or two gazing out my kitchen window in wonder.

Thoughts like these came to me more and more often the longer I lived with a teenaged son. Questions of "Why?" and questions of the universe and endless questions and opinions about how to live in this messed-up culture. I suggested ways of seeing that involved being optimistic and positive, and while he didn't exactly scoff he often became impatient. He needed to be in the forest. He'd said the previous night, for instance, that he had too much energy in his head right now, not enough in his feet.

I SAT AT MY desk, gazing out the window at the first snowfall of the season. Ben and I had shared the morning paper together over coffee before he left for work. I would be joining him downtown later, but for now I was reading a poem on a friend's website, a poem toasting a lifelong friendship. I was hoping for inspiration and just as I began to write, Yeats pressed play on his stereo in the room beside me. Cat Stevens began to sing his song about wanting to last forever, riding the great white bird up to heaven. I felt deeply moved. Not because I wanted to be young again, but because this day marked two anniversaries and the music brought on a flood of nostalgia. I wanted to slow time down.

It was exactly eleven years since I'd begun writing with

The Moving Pen, my weekly writing group. I cherished that writing time and those women who sat around the table every week, bearing witness to our artistic selves. And it was twenty-one years since Dad died. While I didn't dwell on that loss anymore, and it no longer caused me deep grief, it did sit in me somewhere, lightly. Played with me a little.

The passage of time. Here was a song that reminded me of death, and a poem that spoke of love and friendship, and a special day in the calendar year that marked my journey to a deeper self-awareness.

No birds flew past my window. No crow. No falcon. The trees stood naked and swayed in the winter wind, their branches covered in snow. I sat watching the clouds, being in my life, being here now.

FURTHER RESOURCES

BOOKS

Bull, John L., and John Farron, Jr. *Audubon Society Field Guide to North American Birds: Eastern Region*. New York: Knopf, 1977.

Gibson, Graeme. *The Bedside Book of Birds: An Avian Miscellany*. Toronto: Doubleday, 2005.

Howell, Steve N. G. and Jon Dunn. *Gulls of the Americas*. Peterson Field Guides. Boston: Houghton Mifflin Company, 2007.

Hughes, Janice M. *ROM Field Guide to Birds of Ontario*. Toronto: Royal Ontario Museum and McClelland & Steward, 2001.

Matthiessen, Peter. *The Snow Leopard*. New York: Viking, 1978.

National Geographic Field Guide to the Birds of North America. Third Edition. Washington, D.C.: National Geographic Society, 1999.

Sibley, David Allen. *The Sibley Guide to Birds*. New York: Knopf, 2000.

WEBSITES

Amherst Island: www.amherstisland.on.ca

The Cornell Lab of Ornithology: www.allaboutbirds.org

Nature Conservancy of Canada: www.natureconservancy.ca

Pelee Island: www.pelee.org

Point Pelee National Park: www.pc.gc.ca/pn-np/on/pelee/index.aspx

Wye Marsh: http://www.wyemarsh.com

ACKNOWLEDGEMENTS

BIRDING WITH YEATS would not exist without the brilliant vision of Sarah MacLachlan at House of Anansi Press. It was her idea, and I thank her very much for having it and then handing it over to Janie Yoon, my friend and editor. Janie brought the idea to me and now it is a book. Sometimes it feels like that—Janie waved her magic wand and helped me to create a book out of nothing but little stories. But mostly it was hard work and I thank Janie for believing I could write this book and for helping me do it.

Thanks go to everyone else at Anansi, too, for being their wonderful, exuberant selves. A book is a team effort and Anansi is a great team. Special thanks to Alysia Shewchuk for her lovely jacket and map designs, and to Laura Repas, my publicist, for her dedication.